# I. INTRODUCTION.

## A. BACKGROUND.

Latin America's Southern Cone began a process of economic liberalization, democratization, and integration in the late 1980s, almost simultaneous with the end of the Cold War and the rise of the globalization phenomenon. All these elements intertwined, changing the sub-region's insertion in the international system as well as its domestic models of development.

Liberalization began because of the exhaustion of the import-substitution industrialization (ISI) applied in Latin America since the 1929 world recession and because of the 1980s debt crisis. Systematic and coherent liberalization policies began in 1985 in Chile and were adopted in 1990 by Argentina and Brazil. However, countries selected different strategies for liberalization. Chile opted for unilateral opening and "multiple insertion", while Argentina and Brazil regulated their opening through the integration process.

Democratization formally began in 1980 with the democratic election of Peruvian President Fernando Belaúnde Terry, and continued with Bolivia in 1982, Argentina in 1983, Brazil and Uruguay in 1985, Paraguay in 1989, and Chile in 1990.

The integration process began in 1985. President Raúl Alfonsín of Argentina proposed to his new Brazilian colleague José Sarney to develop integration to end the bilateral nuclear competition, but also to stabilize their respective fragile domestic political situations after military regimes. However, integration was consolidated only after both countries committed to liberalization in 1990, which led to the creation of a sub-regional block, the Common Market of the South (whose Spanish acronym is Mercosur), also including Uruguay and Paraguay, which established a free trade zone, a customs union, and a common market. In 1996, Chile became an associate member of Mercosur by signing a bilateral free-trade treaty with the group.

Within this broader context, the change in the Southern Cone includes two extraordinary features, given the sub-regional history. The first is a "Copernican" shift in Southern Cone strategic relationships. This ended a historical pattern of conflict and rivalry enduring since their 19th Century independence period (1810-1829), during which countries had been able to develop significant levels of cooperation among rivals and to create a stable but precarious "zone of peace" (Kacowicz 1998). Countries had been able to peacefully resolve their disputes through the use of international law, but much of this had depended on deterrence strategies and rested on the real possibility of armed inter-state conflict. In contrast, since 1985, the whole sub-region has reached unprecedented levels of security cooperation. Argentina and Brazil assert today that they have eliminated their mutual conflict hypothesis and reached high levels of defense consultation and coordination. In 1999 Chile and Argentina formally resolved their last border disputes, which almost led them to an open war in 1978. In May 2001, the Chilean President visited the Argentine Congress and stated that the bilateral "threat scenario was over forever"[1] and proposed a "strategic alliance" with Argentina, with which Chile shares a common border of about 4,200 kilometers (Lagos 2000: 65).

During this period (1983-2001), countries have adopted cooperative security practices, producing a dense network of regimes in such areas as weapons of mass

---

[1] Lagos' original sentence was that "la hipótesis de conflicto está desechada para siempre".

destruction, as well as an increasingly sophisticated network of bilateral confidence-building measures. In 1998, Mercosur, Chile, and Bolivia declared their combined territories a "Zone of Peace", and countries are exploring a "new agenda" of security cooperation focused on trans-national common security problems (Pérez 1997). Because of these achievements, some authors assert that the Southern Cone is moving toward a "pluralistic security community" (Hurrel 1998a, Barletta 2000).

A second major feature is that Mercosur became a new international actor in the international system. The 1994 Ouro Preto Protocol gave it juridical status, and, because of the creation of the customs union, member countries began to act as a block in international economic negotiations. This happened with Chile's association in 1996 and in the ongoing negotiations for the Free Trade Zone of the Americas (FTAA) and the European Union-Mercosur Free Trade Agreement, while proposals for Mercosur-SADC and Mercosur-ASEAN inter-regional dialogues have been proposed. This is a major change in the Southern Cone strategic situation. For the first time in history, a significant part of Latin America is formally an international actor.

However, the question is whether Mercosur will strengthen its profile as a regional actor in foreign, security, and military affairs. Will the Southern Cone's increasing economic integration and political concertation produce a "spillover effect" into security and military multilateral sub-regional regimes? To date it has not done so. Argentina informally offered proposals for a multinational Southern Cone military force (a "small NATO"), but the idea received an outright and formal negative from Uruguay and a cold silence from Brazil and Chile. During the 1990s the countries have increased their participation in international and regional security regimes and have even

3

strengthened security regimes within the sub-regional but, despite these cooperative impetuses, Southern Cone states also still base their security on their own military capabilities, do not have sub-regional military alliances, have been unlikely to negotiate conventional arms controls, and are reluctant to advance toward supranational military organizations.

## B. RESEARCH QUESTIONS AND THESIS STATEMENT.

This thesis aims to explain Southern Cone security cooperation and the limits to this cooperation. Why did Southern Cone security cooperation regimes suddenly increase during the 1990s? Is there a rationale governing them? How does this rationale explain the form cooperation assumes? How does this rationale shape the political and strategic choices countries have made and must continue to make?

This thesis analyzes the progress in inter-state security cooperation among Argentina, Brazil, and Chile (ABC) since 1983 as a consequence of their adoption of a new model of development shaped by three interrelated variables: political democratization, economic liberalization, and sub-regional integration, the causal role of which has varied during the process.

Argentina's political democratization in 1983, followed by transitions to democracy in Brazil in 1985 and Chile in 1990, originated the push toward security cooperation, ending a long phase of interstate rivalry and opening a second historical period of security cooperation. However, while the politics of democratic consolidation and ideological variables were necessary to initiate cooperation, it is unlikely that they would have been sufficient to sustain it in the long term. This has been the role performed

4

by economic liberalization, adopted by the ABC countries since 1990. Economic liberalization led, for the first time in the countries' history, to growing levels of economic, societal, and political interdependence, which in turn changed the mutual threat perceptions and created incentives for largely bilateral cooperative security practices. Thus, the security cooperation originated on a political and ideological basis was cemented on a material basis.

Finally, deeper economic integration and the creation of a customs union in 1995 have stimulated a more advanced phase of security cooperation, featuring germinal sub-regional multilateral collective action by Mercosur and Chile. However, its consolidation will depend on Mercosur's ability to overcome the crisis of the customs union and to develop a common foreign and security policy, on ABC's common sub-regional threat perception, and on the ability of the ABC's to resolve their currently divergent foreign policies regarding the United States.

The hypothesis argues that security cooperation has been a multi-causal process and stresses the importance of governments, which have acted to regulate the pace and nature of integration and security cooperation, subordinating it to their countries' international insertion but first and foremost to the domestic political stability of their democratic regimes. The thesis highlights that ABC integration has been a strategy deliberately crafted to strengthen Southern Cone states' capacity for governance, both at domestic and international levels.

## C. METHODOLOGICAL ASPECTS.

### 1. Conceptual Framework.

Although integration processes have been ongoing in several regions of the international system since the aftermath of World War II, half a century later the theoretical literature remains very inconclusive, and there is wide scholarly agreement that no school of thought has been able to encompass the whole complexity of the processes. The metaphor of integration as an elephant proposed by Puchala (1972), in which he compared contending theories of integration to the rationalization of blind men who had felt their way around different parts of an elephant, remains valid as a reflection on the methodological problems that complex processes present for their study and is even often quoted.

One dimension of integration's complexity is horizontal. It lies in the holistic character of integration processes. They involve not only different levels of analysis, but also different sectors, including politics, economics, and strategy, among others[2]. Unlike regimes, which can be more narrowly defined, integration is a much more-encompassing process of negotiation in which governments bargain to manage increasing interdependence between countries. They usually simultaneously negotiate a wide range of sectoral agreements, ranging from economics to political decision-making and from peripheral to primary areas of state and societal interests, in a period that, regarding the *tempo* of the states, is relatively short. Despite variations among different processes of

---

[2] For a discussion of the concept of sectors, that is, areas with "specific types of interactions", see Buzan (1998: 7-8) and Helen Wallace (2000: 78).

6

integration, they constitute a negotiation of a complex regime leading to a different type of inter-state and inter-societal coexistence.

The second dimension of integration's complexity is vertical. It lies in the fact that these processes are dynamics simultaneously affected by variables acting at different levels of analysis, according to Waltz's (1959, 1979) classical distinction between the international system, the nation-state, and the individual[3]. At the international level regional integration processes escape neither the consequences of international distribution of power nor the effects of existing international regimes above a regional level. As Hurrel (1995) noted, systemic and neo-realist theories still have something to say about regionalist strategies. For instance, theories of alliance formation continue to illuminate not only the ways in which countries balance within a region, but also the dynamics introduced by external hegemonic actors (Walt 1987). Others have underlined the importance of an adequate intra-regional distribution of the economic, political, and strategic gains that can emerge from cooperation (Grieco 1988). However, realist schools of thought[4] say little about the role of variables other than power and/or threats[5], and since the 1980s, with the rise of the neo-liberal scholarly literature, many scholars have proposed that integration processes must be understood as international regime building, an argument that is currently widely accepted[6].

---

[3] For more recent, non-structural-realist definitions incorporating new levels of analysis and actors, see Dougherty and Pfaltzgraff Jr. (1997: 27-31), Buzan (1998: 5-6) and Levy (1999: 4).

[4] For a recent detailed discussion on the differences between different realist schools of thought see Jervis 1999.

[5] Traditional and structural realist theories shared a common concern about distribution of states' capabilities within the international system and their seeking for power, but Stephen Walt (1987) innovated by underlining the importance of threat and the states' quest for security.

[6] The standard definition understands international regimes as a "set of implicit or explicit principles, norms, rules, and decision-making procedures around which actors' expectations converge" in a given area

Therefore, methodologically integration falls within the scope of international relations theory, but at the same time, as Moravcsik suggests, integration pertains to foreign policy analysis[7] because the empirical evidence shows a strong link between processes at the regional level, especially those aimed at integration, and domestic politics[8]. According to several scholars, states shape their behavior in two successive stages. "Governments first define a set of interests, then bargain among themselves in an effort to realize those interests" (Moravcsik 1993: 481). However, the processes are also two-way streets: by facilitating strategies that allow leaders to address problems at domestic levels, in turn regional regimes have evidenced capacity to become intervening variables at a level other than the international (Keohane and Hoffman 1991: 25). Therefore, integration studies also need to understand the interactions between the domestic and international levels.

---

of international relations (Krasner 1982, 1983: 2). Hoffman proposed the first theorization of integration as regimes and according to him, "the best way of analyzing the European Economic Community (EEC) is not in the traditional terms of integration theory, which assumes that members are engaged in the formation of a new, supranational political entity superseding the old nations (...). It is to look at the EEC as an international regime, as defined by Keohane and Nye: a set of norms of behavior and of rules and policies covering a broad range of issues, dealing both with procedures and with substance, and facilitating agreements among the members" (Hoffmann 1982: 33). Moravcsik refined Hoffmann and argued that European integration is "a successful intergovernmental regime designed to manage economic interdependence through negotiated policy co-ordination", a theory that rests "on the assumption that state behavior reflects the rational actions of governments constrained at home by domestic societal pressures and abroad by their strategic environment" (1993: 474). Hoffmann's approach has been widely accepted, and while the concept of regime has been enriched, the debate has focused on which are the most important variables shaping regimes (Hasenclever *et al* 1997).

[7] For the traditional and contested distinction between the studies of foreign policy and international relations see Waltz 1979 (121-2).

[8] For other similar approaches on European integration see Keohane and Hoffman (1991) and Sandholtz and Zyman (1989).

Therefore, integration processes pervade both the horizontal and vertical dimensions[9], which are usually analyzed separately for methodological reasons, but which conform a single reality in the "real world". Because of this complexity and the difficulties in understanding (not to mention predicting) integration processes, scholarly research has exhibited a twofold trend. On the one hand it has become more focused on partial aspects of the processes (McCormick 1999, Nugent 1999, Puchala 1998, Wallace 2000b). On the other hand, as explained before, integration research has been subsumed by mainstream International Relations theory, especially by regime theory (Wallace 2000:68-70). However, at the same time, these trends have created a theoretical vacuum by default. As Putnam noted, while theories began to emphasize interdependence and transnationalism, "the role of domestic factors slipped more and more out of focus, particularly as the concept of international regimes came to dominate the subfield" (Putnam 1988: 43).

Faced with this theoretical vacuum, some scholars have pursued "mid-range" explanations, trying to articulate theories and variables acting both "vertically" and "horizontally". Liberal intergovernmentalism, articulated by Moravcsik (1991, 1993, 1995), has been one attempt. It draws from international regimes theory and Putnam's two-level game theory of international politics, asserting that the European integration process must be essentially understood as a bargain between governments keeping one eye on domestic politics and the other on international politics and being able to govern (and therefore to express sovereignty) through regimes which, when perceived as consolidated, can even be managed by supranational institutions. In this sense, Moravcsik

---

[9] Wallace uses a similar analytical framework –"vertical and horizontal pathways"-- in her comparative study of integration theories. See Wallace (2000: 77-80).

has made a significant contribution. He did not "reject" current mainstream international relations theories (like Keohane's regime theory and Putnam two-level game theory). Instead, he was able to integrate them, assuming that each one was explaining a part of the phenomenon, and through the articulation of variables and theories acting at different levels he was able to provide an explanation for a specific process, European integration. That is, "although the EU [European Union] is a unique institution, it does not require a *sui generis* theory" (1993: 474)

Wallace's theory of collective governance has been another attempt. It shares several similarities with Moravcsik, particularly in relation to the need to understand the European Union as a phenomenon that simultaneously integrates different levels of analysis. However, contrary to Moravcsik, who considers the states as the main actors, Wallace concludes that the EU "is a collective political system, not an intergovernmental regime" (2000: 530). "States, as represented by central governments, remain central to the EU policy process but they are no longer the *only* significant actors and not always the predominant actors" (2000: 532). Their actions are constrained by the European and national institutional frameworks and actors playing simultaneously at multiple levels, making Europe a partial polity with a system of collective governance through consociational elite institutions in which policy-making "may thus be described as post-sovereign" (2000: 533).

Finally, and following the early works of Karl Deutsch (1957) and the "Yale Group" (Mally 1973: 37), constructivist theories of international relations also pay special attention to regionalist dynamics and integration processes, for they observe the potential emergence of a singular, distinctive phenomenon resulting from integration

10

processes: "the possibility that, at some point [...] it might lead to the emergence of a cohesive and consolidated regional unit" (Hurrel 1995: 44-5)-- that is, to the deliberate creation of polities or communities other than the state within the international system, able to produce peaceful changes "through the institutionalization of mutual identification, transnational values, intersubjective understandings, and shared identities" (Adler and Barnett 1998b: 58, 1998a)[10].

Despite their differences, constructivists share some commonalities with liberal intergovernmentalists, or collective governance proponents: their approaches overcome the artificial (although methodologically legitimate) division of levels of analysis to analyze a phenomenon such as integration that, to be understood as a whole needs that methodological step.

The process of integration in South America is as complex as the European process, but the region's experience has received less scholarly attention in comparative terms. In part this is because integration has been less systematic than in Europe. The first attempt began during the 1950s but were quickly interrupted or neutralized, and the second moment is relatively recent. In the first phase, early functionalist but especially neo-functionalist European theories of integration[11] were influential in Latin American

---

[10] It is also worth noting that, such as Liberal intergovernmentalism and other theories, constructivist theories are not limited to integration processes and, on the contrary, propose a more general interpretation of international politics, understanding it not only as resulting from power relations and material interests, but also as a social construction in which ideational factors play a crucial role. See Wendt 1992.

[11] The main earlier European theories of integration after World War II were functionalism (Mitrany 1965) and neo-functionalism (Haas 1958, Lindberg 1963, Lindberg and Scheingold, 1971). The main proposition of neo-functionalism was the coining of the concept of "spillover" –"the material logic of the facts on integration urges us relentlessly on from one step to the next, from one field to another" (Nye 1971: 65)- to describe the main dynamic behind integration processes toward the creation of supra-national power center. However, one of the main conclusions since the 1965 European Community crisis was that spillover was neither mechanical nor unaffected by other domestic or international political events. Also, instead being studied as a process toward a federal entity, European integration began to be studied more as

formulations of the regional agenda for integration, although the final Latin American formulation presented important differences. While in Central America the neo-functionalist European model was followed in a more orthodox way (Nye 1971), its South American version, elaborated by the United Nations Economic Commission for Latin America (Klarén 1986: 15), differed from the European theories of integration because "it put more emphasis on the commercial aspects of the process than on its implications for infrastructure and the productive sectors, and -within this perspective- on intra-regional trade rather than on external economic relations" (Tomassini 1985: 215)[12].

The 1990's process of integration has been the subject of a far more rich and varied scholarship, with extensive research focusing on several different parts of its "vertical" and "horizontal" dimensions. For instance, and without pretending an exhaustive overview, several aspects of the former dimension have been studied. The relationship with the international system (Jaguaribe 1998, Rojas 1998), the construction of regional regimes (Varas 1993, 1994, Rojas 1994), the impact of regional processes on domestic politics (Valenzuela 1997, Guilhon 1999), and the domestic dynamics leading to foreign policies (Van Klaveren 1996) are some of the levels that have been analyzed. Sectoral studies have also received considerable attention. Because of its centrality, economics has been among the privileged areas (ECLAC 1994, Manzetti 1993-94, Roett 1999, Zahler 1999), but security has also received close attention (Fuentes 1997, Rojas 1999, Hurrel 1998, Barletta 1999, 2000, Fournier 1999), among other sectors.

---

an international regime (Hoffmann 1982:33), which to be successful depended on a prior intergovernmental bargain (Keohane and Hoffmann 1991).

[12] For earlier non-Latin American attempts to encompass the region's integration experiences see Etzioni (1965), Haas (1966), Nye (1971), and Tomassini (1985). For recent attempts see Nishijima and Smith (1996), Anderson (1999), Hurrell (1997).

However, as in the European case, much of the research on Latin American integration aims at particular dimensions of the process, and little of it tries to address whether it does have a more general logic articulating and providing sense, order, and direction through the different sectors and levels of analysis.

As the hypothesis proposes, this thesis aims to essay an interpretation of the Argentine, Brazilian, and Chilean security relationships within the process of integration, and to propose an explanation of how the process is governed and how this governance at the regional level is able to integrate variables acting vertically (at different levels of analysis) and horizontally (in different sectors). Thus, the thesis aims at a mid-range scope. Given the above-explained complexity of integration experiments, it will proceed by analyzing the main variables in the cases under study. Paraphrasing Hurrell (1985: 71-3), the thesis will explore two different but complementary options. First, it will claim that to understand integration processes it is not necessary to claim the primacy of some specific theory. On the contrary, the thesis asserts that it is necessary to "explore the nature of the interaction between different logics that we see at work" in regional integration -economic, political, and security-, each of which has been previously explained by specific theories. Second, it asserts that it is even useful to adopt a "staged-theory" approach to understanding integration, that is, a process through which the causal role of variables or even the usefulness of theories may vary over time. Following Puchala's metaphor, the thesis claims that each blind man has a valid but limited knowledge about part of the elephant, but assembling their dispersed knowledge and, moreover, studying how the parts change over time produces a better picture.

## 2. Case Selection. Why Study Argentina, Brazil, and Chile?

There are several reasons to select two full Mercosur members (Argentina and Brazil) and one associated member (Chile). First, the Southern Cone has traditionally been an interstate sub-system within South America, exhibiting analytically distinguishable international relations with it and with the international system. According to Atkins, this sub-system features a "relative isolation from the mainstream of international politics, largely a function of its unique geographic situation" and its relatively high level of institutionalization and state strength. This "has left the region free, for the most part, from inclusion in global balance-of-power rivalries and helped it resist outside influences in the handling of internal affairs". Because of this, and in stark contrast to northern Latin America, the ABC's have established "independent patterns of interaction involving their own set of sub-regional issues" (Atkins 1995: 33), in which:

> Sub-regional international relations have brought strategic-geopolitical components to the foreign policies of the major Southern Cone states. They have developed such calculations primarily in regard to their own sub-region, extended to include the South Atlantic and the Antarctic (Atkins 1995: 33) [13].

Secondly, the 1990s integration process did not involve all the Southern Cone actors with the same intensity. Integration among Argentina, Brazil, and Chile was deeper and created a new strategic situation with unprecedented by strong economic flows in both directions between the Atlantic and the Pacific. This dynamic has reinforced the traditional distinctiveness of the ABC within South America[14] and,

---

[13] Several other authors also consider the Western South Pacific coast as part of the sub-system (Burr 1967, Cañas 1956).

[14] Chile's 1996 association to Mercosur benefited the group with a wider, global outlook because of Chile's strong links with the Asia-Pacific economies. Governments' policy makers have perceived this new dynamic. As noted by Peña, a former Undersecretary of Trade at the Argentine Ministry of Economic

therefore, the usefulness of its study. Thus, the thesis will include three of the four main countries that traditionally constituted the Southern Cone sub-system. Peru will not be included because in spite of its accelerated unilateral liberalization since the 1990s, until 2001 the country had not participated in the integration process. Thus, Peru will remain as a relevant strategic actor but is not useful in comparative terms for the purposes of this study.

### 3. Relevance of the Study.

Security relations in the Southern Cone are evolving rapidly, and most studies focus on their initial stages. Some have also emphasized partial aspects, especially the Argentine-Brazilian relationship, but few have adopted a sub-regional perspective between the bilateral and the hemispheric or international levels.

The topic is also important in political and strategic terms. South America has been one of the most stable regions in the world during the 19th and 20th centuries. It is in the interest of the international community to know whether under the new conditions the region will maintain this feature or will be unstable or conflict prone.

---

Affairs during the Menem administration, through these countries "runs a corridor including twenty large cities, from the triangle formed by Belo Horizonte, Río de Janeiro, and Sao Paulo in the north to Montevideo, Buenos Aires, and Santiago in the South. This corridor contains some seventy million urban consumers with a per capita income about US$ 10,000. From an economic point of view, that corridor is the nucleus of Mercosur's consumption and production" (Peña 1999: 54), and the most dynamic Latin American economic focus. According to Jorge Castro, a former Argentine Presidency's Secretary for Strategic Planning, before the creation of Mercosur and the Chilean association to the group, Argentine exports had to be transported from the interior to Buenos Aires and then to their foreign markets. After these two events, they are not restricted to flow only throughout the Plata Basin. Today they can go directly from northern Argentina to Brazil's Atlantic, and from southern Argentina to the Pacific through Chile's seaports. "This time, the effort for international insertion aims at the main axis of world growth: the Asia-Pacific" (Castro 1998: 43).

Finally, this thesis may eventually contribute to better understanding of the dynamics and consequences of the current international regionalist trend, a field that remains very inconclusive despite decades of theorizing.

## 4. Thesis Organization.

The thesis will proceed in three steps, applying both historical and comparative methods to study the process of integration and security cooperation, and will then make a concluding assessment. Chapter II studies the long period of security rivalries between ABC countries produced by models of development that shared low levels of interdependence. This phase ranges from the ABC states' formative period, through19th century liberalism, to 20th century Import-Substitution, which ended as a model during the 1980s. For this purpose this chapter will make a comparative analysis between the four basic Southern Cone models of development (1810/mid 1800s, late 1800s/1929, 1929/1983, 1983/2001) to assess how they produced a distinctive strategic outcome. The factors this comparison will include are the international context, domestic political regimes, and economic strategies (Post independence, Laissez Faire, ISI), and the levels of interdependence among Argentina, Brazil, and Chile (1810-1983).

Chapter III covers the period in which inter-state relationships changed toward increased security cooperation and conflict prevention regimes, aiming to address the international system, domestic political regimes, and economic strategies of development, including regional integration as a central part of states' strategies. These variables led to a change in the inter-state strategic relationships. To assess the strategic changes, it will make a comparative analysis of the defense policies and military capabilities of the ABC.

Chapter IV focuses on the prospects for further and deepened regimes of security cooperation within the integration process, especially regarding under what conditions a sub-regional regime of security cooperation could strengthen the states' domestic political stability, their transition from ISI to market economies, and their relationship with the international system.

Finally, Chapter V summarizes conclusions and assesses the findings regarding the eventual need for further research and different theorization, as the above conceptual framework suggests.

THIS PAGE INTENTIONALLY LEFT BLANK

## II. MODELS OF DEVELOPMENT AND INTERSTATE RELATIONS, 1810-1983: FROM POST-INDEPENDENCE COOPERATION, TO COMPETITION, TO A STABLE BUT PRECARIOUS ZONE OF PEACE.

This chapter will focus on explaining the security relationships that Argentina, Brazil, and Chile developed in the Southern Cone until the late 1980s, the "stable zone of negative peace"[15] based on deterrence and conflict management regimes, which preceded the late 1980s' and early 1990s' shift toward conflict prevention regimes, common or cooperative security[16] practices, and -according to some authors- security community building (Hurrel 1998a). For this purpose, the chapter will examine three periods that roughly correspond to what the standard scholarly literature considers the main phases of South (and Latin) American development until the 1990s. In each period, the analysis will pay special attention to how the international system defined the features of the models of development and how each model's political and economic components produced a particular strategic outcome.

---

[15] Kacowicz defines zone of negative peace as a region in which "peace is maintained only on an unstable basis by threats, deterrence, or a lack of will or capabilities to engage in violent conflicts at a certain time" (1998: 9, 60).

[16] The cooperative security concept must be carefully used because, since its origins in the Independent Commission for Disarmament and Security Issues (1982), it has been developed within different contexts and goals. For instance, the Palme Commission (1992) emphasized its potential for European stability, while the Carter, Perry, and Steinbruner (1992) proposal was conceived more as a U.S. post-Cold War hegemonic strategy. In Latin America, the conceptualization offered by cooperative security was welcomed in scholarly circles (Varas 1994b, Rojas 1994), but at governmental and military levels the U.S. proposition to seek hemispheric cooperative regimes formulated by Secretary of Defense William Perry at the 1995 Defense Ministerial conference held at Williamsburg, Virginia, was received with distrust. In 1998, three years later, the Second Summit of the Americas held at Santiago recognized the lack of agreement (Summit of the Americas 1998). For a critical theoretical analysis of the practical shortcomings of applying cooperative security under extreme asymmetric conditions such as those of the U.S.-Latin American relations, see Mares (1994), who draws heavily in Grieco (1988).

The historical patterns of Southern Cone inter-state relations were based on a twofold dynamic: First, for Latin America, during this period the main feature of the international system lay in its hegemonic nature, organized around the British Empire, which successfully replaced Spain as the predominant capitalist core (Kennedy 1976), and later around the United States. Countries directly linked their economic activity with the core countries of the capitalist system, not with the sub-region. The Southern Cone economies never oriented their production for consumption within neighboring countries, which resulted in very low levels of communications and, in a general sense, low interdependence.

Second, the structuring of an increasing inter-state rivalry in the process of nation building complemented this absence of significant economic and societal links between countries. The origins of this process were basically two:

1) The frictions derived from the imprecise jurisdictional borders between the post-independence states inherited from the colonial administrative divisions, which were stabilized only in the late 19th century.

2) The geopolitical competition for land, resources, and lines of communication among the Southern Cone states, as means for assuring each state of its own security and international economic insertion.

The result was an inter-state relations system based on a profound structural mutual distrust, strategic rivalry, and the emergence of a balance of power system, but also one that exhibited a surprising capacity to reach partial but important levels of cooperation. These were partial, because countries perceived themselves as potential, if not real, enemies, but important because in spite of these conditions they were able to develop state behavior featuring common satisfaction with the territorial status quo, the observance of the principle of non-intervention, and the pacific settlement of disputes, including recourse to international arbitration mechanisms[17]. Countries gradually began to develop a regime[18], that is, a set of principles and norms, rules and procedures, that, in general, has prevailed ever since in the region.

Three periods can be distinguished. The first phase (1810-mid 1800s) gave rise to two sub-regional systems of balance of power, one in the Pacific, organized around Chile and Peru, and other in the Atlantic, around Argentina and Brazil. During the second period (late 1800s-1929) both rivalries produced a South American sub-system articulated upon the Argentine-Peruvian and Brazilian-Chilean alliances, but also a conflict prevention regime. The third period (1929-1983) basically consolidated the strategic outcome forged during the late 19th century.

## A. POST-INDEPENDENCE. STRUCTURING VERTICAL TENSIONS IN THE ATLANTIC AND THE PACIFIC, 1810-MID 1800S.

### 1. International Framework.

The history of the Southern Cone emancipation is also a narrative of British success in eroding the Spanish Empire, whose decisive turning point was Napoleon's invasion of Spain, which precipitated -among others things- two relevant consequences for the American Spanish colonies.

---

[17] It is worth noting that this assessment of international relations in the Southern Cone, despite is being widely recognized in the region, is not widely recognized in the mainstream IR scholarly literature, which shortcoming has been noted by students of Third World international relations (Holsti 1992, Neumann 1998). However, recent studies have pointed out this exceptional characteristic of the Southern Cone sub-region. The more elaborated theoretical analysis of this process can be found in Kacowicz (1998). Also, some successful, recently developed security regimes, such as the Association of Southeast Asian Nations (ASEAN), are engineering their relationships precisely trying to reach what the Southern Cone has been able to do since the 19th century. See Acharya (1998), and Alagappa (1998a, 1998b, 1998c).

[18] We refer to Krasner's definition (1982: 186, 1983: 2).

First and foremost, it brought the collapse of the previously declining and still mostly feudal Spanish Empire and, after the victory of the European Concert, uncontested British hegemony over the world, including Spanish Latin America.

Second, it led to the independence wave in this region, although this was born and restricted by the features of the international system imposed by the new hegemon (Burns 1994: 67-126, Skidmore and Smith 1997: 28-41). As Burns points out, after independence "the trend established during the colonial period to subordinate the economy to Europe's needs continued unaltered (…). Dependency accelerated rather than diminished" (Burns 1994: 101, 161), making backwardness a permanent and systemic feature. Without post-independence Latin American neo-colonial exploitation and modes of political domination, modernity would not have been reached in Europe (Rouquié 1987: 23-9). The British domination (and European competence for controlling the region) had an initial phase during which London tried to annex the former Spanish territories. However, Britain was militarily defeated in Buenos Aires (in 1807-8) and Mexico (1808), and so shifted its strategy toward hegemonic neo-colonial domination. Trade was liberalized, and Latin Americans could export and import to and from different centers, but Britain prevented other European powers from colonization and profited from its undisputed naval mastery to control the region (Atkins 1977: 81-4).

Beyond Britain, other non-South American powers intervening in the region were France and the Netherlands in the Caribbean, Portugal in Brazil, and the United States. Washington initially was highly concerned about the British return to the Americas and developed an active diplomacy throughout the region in order to encourage nationalist movements, but later gradually evolved toward a more ambitious strategy partially expressed in 1823 by the U.S. President Monroe[19].

Among the main consequences in this period for the Southern Cone countries was their birth as a dependent but active part of the international system, which imposed restrictions on but also opened opportunities to the strategies the new states could pursue. However, these relationships were also contradictory, because the new nations also experienced traumatic relations with Britain and the other European powers, strengthening South American nationalism.

## 2. The Domestic Framework. Politics and Economics.

Despite the different timing and particular, even contrasting conditions in which each process began, all the new political entities experienced a first period of internal instability and disputes between the different Creole factions over political domination. Brazil experienced a stable pattern of regime transition in 1824 after a conflictive period between monarchists and republicans. Argentina overcame the struggle between unitarians and federalists in 1852. In the Pacific, the earlier stabilization of Chile in 1830 gave the country a competitive and strategic advantage over its rising rival, the former Viceroyalty of Peru, whose stabilization was possible only in 1845. In all of these cases, political regimes were founded upon authoritarian oligarchic regimes.

---

[19] In fact, the first formal signal of concern that led to an active U.S. involvement in the region was the U.S. Congress' No Transfer Resolution of 1811 (Atkins 1977: 113). Despite its visibility, the Monroe Doctrine had few and limited consequences for the region as the U.S. entered its period of civil war, and was used again only in the late 19th century. For more detailed historical studies see Atkins (1977) and Smith (2000).

The length of this period in each new country was decisive. Timing had political and, moreover, strategic effects. In post-independence South America, Chile and Brazil became the hegemons in the Pacific and the Atlantic regions, respectively.

During this period all the states adopted a similar dependent economic model based on exports of raw materials to and imports of processed goods from Britain. Second, as a result of the neo-colonial model, the main Southern Cone communication flows were vertical with the capitalist core, not horizontal within the region, especially not across the Andean cordillera, which was the most formidable physical obstacle to communications in the sub-region. "Trade among the former colonies was also greatly reduced. Northwest Argentina, for instance, suffered from the loss of trade with Peru (...). Communications systems within and between the former colonies, never much favored by the Spaniards, fell into near-total disuse" (Skidmore and Smith 1997: 36). On the Pacific Coast, links were stronger because of the active Colombian and Chilean role in the Peruvian liberation war. What followed was a foreign debt for Peru, and the significant levels of trade inherited from the colonial past (Burr 1967: 22-3, St John 1992: 16-7).

On the other hand, trade with Europe, particularly with Britain, abruptly multiplied. Argentina tripled its trade between 1825-50, and the number of ships sailing from Chile to England rose from three per year in the 1815-20 period to 300 in 1847, especially after the introduction of the steamship on this route, which made the passage of Cape Horn a secure business after 1822 (Burns 1994: 101). In other words, if Chilean trade with Peru was significant, that with England was indispensable, and the same was true for Brazil, Argentina, and even the troubled Peru. Early in the 1820s, London became Peru's main creditor, along with Colombia and Chile (St. John 1992: 16).

### 3. Strategic Outcomes.

The previously explained features of the post-independence period had consequences. They structured the two "perpendicular tensions" of the sub-system, one in the Atlantic, and the other in the Pacific: Brazil/Argentina, and Chile/Peru.

Tensions between Argentina and Brazil exploded in 1825 around the dispute over control of the Rio de la Plata Basin. The Brazilian government became alarmed over the strength and intentions of the Argentine dictator Juan Manuel de Rosas, "who was claiming the right to control all traffic on the Rio de La Plata" (Skidmore and Smith 1997: 152). As a result, Argentina and Brazil fought wars in 1825-28, creating Uruguay as a buffer state; between 1836 and 1852 involving different factions of those three countries; and in 1865-1870, the War of the Triple Alliance (Argentina, Brazil and Uruguay) against Paraguay.

Tensions between Chile and Peru grew as a consequence of a complex process, but mainly after the main ports of Chile and Peru, Valparaíso and Callao respectively, became rivals for the trade between the Atlantic and the Pacific. The emerging rivalry was also prompted by Lima's projects to rebuild its domination over its former vice-royal captaincies of Chile and Bolivia (Burr 1967: 22-57, St John 18-34), and by the then-Alto Peru regime, which aimed to rebuild the Inca Empire through the Peruvian-Bolivian Confederation. The consequence was the Chilean War against the Peruvian-Bolivian Confederation (1836-39), which secured the early Chilean hegemony on the Pacific (Burr 1967).

As Burr argued, during this first phase South America structured two independent sub-systems of balance of power. One was based on the Rio de la Plata Basin: Brazil, Uruguay, Argentina, and Paraguay. The other was on the Pacific Coast: Chile, Peru, Alto Peru (Bolivia), Ecuador, and New Granada (Colombia) (Burr 1967: 20, 32)[20]. This strategic outcome was, as we have seen, articulated around control of the sea-lanes of communication, which were vital to the periphery-core economic relationship.

## B. LATE 19TH CENTURY TO 1929. STRUCTURING THE SOUTHERN CONE "DIAGONAL ALLIANCES".

During the second half of the 19th century the Southern Cone countries experienced three significant changes. The first important feature was the consolidation of the integration of the Latin American countries into the international system, both politically and economically, leading to the period of Latin American modernization. The second feature was the gradual emergence of the U.S. as the new hemispheric hegemon. The third was the structuring of Latin America (and especially South America), like an international subsystem with its own balance of power, relatively marginalized from the great powers' strategic areas of priority. Great powers played a significant strategic role, but were not active military players. However, in response to their pressure, South American countries vigorously promoted the adoption of regional codes of conduct aiming to ameliorate foreign powers' intervention.

### 1. International Framework.

"After 1850 Latin America moved from the post-independence consolidation phase to begin laying the foundations for its greater integration into the world economy"

---

[20] What is of further interest, and one of the merits of Burr, is that he also documented the explicit embracing of the balance of power doctrine by the Chilean elite in the 1830s (Burr 1967: 30-57).

(Skidmore and Smith 1997: 40), a process that "coincided with the extension and intensification of the industrial revolution in Europe and the United States and with the concomitant [...] growing rivalry for markets to export manufactured products, and sources of raw materials" (Burr 1967: 109). As the dependent part of the system, South America was deeply engaged in the core of the long period of world economic expansion and liberalism that ended only with the international crisis of 1929.

Britain became the predominant actor in the Southern Cone. Economically, "between 1870 and 1913 the value of Britain's investments in Latin America went from 85 million pounds sterling to 757 million pounds", almost two-thirds of total foreign investment in the region, as Britain assumed control of Latin American economies and deepened the dependent pattern established by Spain.

Thus, Britain became significantly interdependent with the Southern Cone and, therefore, highly interested in regional and local politics. However, her strategy in the region was very close to her European practice of being the "balancer" of continental power balances (Kennedy 1976). As will be seen below, she played an active role, administering the balance in South America and trying to prevent European competition (mostly from the rising German and Italian powers after the 1870s) and U.S. emergence as the hegemon in the Hemisphere after the Monroe Doctrine.

Second, from the late 19th and early 20th centuries the Southern Cone experienced the second major shift in its international insertion as the consequence of changes in the international system, whose main features were the decline of the British Empire and the gradual emergence of the United States as the new hegemonic power in America. Both processes are interrelated, but they need to be analyzed separately because they are analytically different and, moreover, had different impacts on the Southern Cone.

The construction of the U.S. hegemony in the Americas was accelerated from the late 19th century by two dynamics. The basic one was the economic and geographic expansion of the U.S., leading to the materialization of the "Manifest Destiny" doctrine (the U.S. expansion from coast to coast) and its rise as a naval power in the Atlantic and the Pacific. The second main factor was the strategic dilemma that the U.S. and Germany's expansion posed to Britain from 1870 to 1914, which led to the gradual British withdrawal from the Americas because of the impossibility of sustaining a two-front strategy given the deteriorating European situation (Kennedy 1977, Layne 1994: 196-9, Smith 2000: 31).

The main outcome was the resurrection of the Monroe Doctrine more than half a century after its proclamation. Strategically, the U.S. geopolitical strategy now included the Caribbean basin as an area of vital interests to be preserved, leading to an intense period of dispute with the European powers in this sub-region, especially with the United Kingdom. The British withdrawal began in 1850 with the Clayton-Bulwer Treaty allowing the United States to build and exclusively control an interoceanic canal (Atkins 1977: 85), continued with the Trent Affair (Layne 1994: 187-93), and reached its point of no return in the Venezuelan crisis of 1895-6, in which London "tacitly" recognized the "claim to American preeminence throughout the Western Hemisphere [...]. Through the Venezuelan controversy, the United States had taken a major step toward the achievement of de facto hegemony in the Americas" (Smith 2000: 31-2, Layne 1994: 193-99). After that Britain began to retreat from the Americas, "retaining major interests in South America [...], especially concentrated in Argentina and Brazil". A few years later, in 1904, U.S. President Theodore Roosevelt stated his "Roosevelt Corollary" to the Monroe Doctrine explicitly claiming "the right to intervene (invade) Latin American nations" (Bagby 1999: 67). Finally, in the 1919 Versailles Peace Conference the very liberal U.S. President Woodrow Wilson championed the principle of self-determination for national minorities in the defeated empires in EuropeHowever,

> The British and French colonial empires were treated as single political units [....]. At the behest of the American delegation, the Monroe Doctrine was specifically excluded from the purview of the League Covenant (thereby preserving the exclusive prerogative of the United States to maintain the peace in its hemisphere) (Keylor 1996: 74).

Nevertheless, Latin America's importance for the Unites States was not only geopolitical, but also economic. Washington policymakers and Congressmen were conscious that after the U.S. Civil War, in order to sustain economic growth and avoid the economic depression cycles that had devastated the economy in 1873-78, 1882-85, and 1893-97, U.S. products and surplus capital needed new markets for sales and investment, and Latin America was seen as critical in this context (Smith 2000: 28-29).

Therefore, the U.S. hegemony that became a reality for Europeans only after World War II, had been a reality for Latin Americans several decades before, despite different intensities depending on the sub-region, and it was felt both economically and militarily.

Militarily, the U.S. used military force more than thirty times in the Caribbean basin between 1898 and 1934 (Bagby 1999: 67, Smith 2000: 50-51), while in the Southern Cone it exercised an increasing gunboat diplomacy aiming to consolidate its hemispheric hegemony regarding Britain's remaining influence. The U.S. openly intervened during the War of the Pacific favoring Peru because Chile was perceived as aligned with Great Britain, threatening the former with the use of force in 1881 after the Chilean occupation of Lima (Burr 1967: 156-7), and bilateral tensions arose in 1891 after the incident of the *USS Baltimore* in the Chilean seaport of Valparaíso (Smith 2000: 30). Washington's military support for Peru continued during the early 20th century, the U.S. serving as last Peruvian guarantor in case of a failure in the settlement of the Tacna-Arica question, because of U.S. concerns regarding the Chilean naval power, and Japan's and Britain's strong naval relations with Chile. However, after the pending Chilean-Peruvian issues were resolved through the 1929 Lima Protocols, U.S. conflict hypotheses with Chile were maintained at least until 1933 (Meneses 1993: 371-2).

Third, strategically speaking the South American region consolidated a particular feature within the international system, already assuming worldwide dimensions: the region came under hegemonic domination, but at the same time it was marginalized from the great powers' areas of vital strategic interests. At the same time, it structured a balance of power system and enjoyed a relatively high level of institutionalization that "helped her to resist outside influences in the handling of internal affairs" (Atkins 1977: 33, 84).

## 2. Domestic Framework. (Partial) Political, and (full) Economic Liberalization.

Regarding domestic environments, this is the period of sub-regional stabilization, mostly through oligarchic authoritarian regimes that gradually introduced democratic institutions.

This occurred in Peru with the Ramón Castilla regime in 1845, and also in Argentina with the defeat of Rosas and the consolidation of the federal, liberal republic

30

after 1852 under Bartolomé Mitre's leadership. Having clear leadership and internal order, both countries began to exercise active, coherent foreign policies in their respective sub-systems, which meant their full emergence as regional actors and, therefore, a shift in the current regional balances. As Burr explained, the almost simultaneous processes of consolidation of Argentina and Peru as nation-states from the mid-1800s led to their alliance during the 1870s and, thus, to the "integration into a single system of the previously separate Platine and Pacific regional systems of power politics" (Burr 1967: 107). Political stabilization, in this sense, had strong strategic consequences.

This is also the period during which the South American countries tried to fully adopt the ideological, political, and economic institutions of modernity. Political regimes inspired by North American presidentialism and federalism, or by European parliamentarism, were gradually adopted.

Economic liberalism was also adopted. These were the years of the export booms in Chile and Brazil, but also in Argentina and Peru, which led to the processes of modernization, industrialization, and the consolidation of positivism as the natural evolution from the Enlightenment. However, as Burns has also noted, "the export sector of the Latin American economy grew more rapidly than the domestic sector, and income from foreign trade contributed an unusually high percentage of the of the gross national product. Foreign trade emphatically did not mean commerce among Latin American states. They were strangers in each other's marketplaces. Their economies complemented the demands of the distant major capitalistic economies in Western Europe and the United States" (Burns 1994: 144).

### 3. Strategic Outcomes.

Economic modernization also had strategic effects in South America. With different timing, countries began to realize the economic value of regions of the continent hitherto neglected. When the Bolivian and Peruvian governments turned to the Atacama Desert to exploit the guano and, later, the nitrate fields, they realized that Chilean-British capital had been there for many years, even under legal authorizations given by La Paz. For several reasons, subsequent negotiations were unable to reach an agreement, leading to a crisis that escalated in 1879 into the War of the Pacific.

Equally, when the Argentines turned back to the south seeking land for cattle and wool, they discovered that Chile was also there, claiming control over the Magellan Strait in the far south, which was of critical strategic importance for the Atlantic-Pacific trade and for Valparaíso, which after the 1836 war was consolidated as the unavoidable port on the route to California from the gold rush until the construction of the Panama Canal. In the Platine basin, competition for navigation routes not only increased but also expanded to the Amazon basin after the surge of the world demand for rubber, leading to structural tension between Brazil and its Amazonian neighbors, including Peru.

The final outcome of these disputes in the Southern Cone was profound, structuring South America's definitive, modern boundaries. In the Atlantic sub-system, Brazil, allied with Uruguay and Argentina, defeated Paraguay as an emerging power in the 1865-70 war, while the post-1870s Argentina's rise as a regional power confirmed its rivalry with Brazil. In the Pacific sub-system, tensions grew leading to the War of the Pacific in 1879, after which Chile extended its territories to the Peruvian province of Tarapacá and the Bolivian province of Antofagasta. In the South, Chile extended its formal jurisdiction to Cape Horn, diplomatically settling its border and territorial disputes with Argentina, but not without a significant military competition that was moderated only in 1902 with the Pactos de Mayo. This agreement ended the bilateral arms (mainly naval) race and established the spheres of influence that would rule their relationship since then: Chile in the Pacific, and Argentina in the Atlantic. Before that, the two countries, by then governed by democratic regimes, had been on the verge of war in 1898 and 1901.

The period of modernization also had further strategic consequences because the aftermath of the War of the Pacific led to the professionalization of the military. The Argentine, Chilean, and even Brazilian governments contracted Prussian military missions to train and reform their armies, importing modern military institutions and the Prussian military geopolitical thought of the late 19th and early 20th centuries (Nunn 1976: 83-172, Rouquié 1987: 72-97, Child 1990: 58). The consequence was the structuring of what today could be called a South American epistemic military community of mutual rivalry. This enmity was cemented during the 20th century by the persistence of inter-state rivalries and border disputes inherited from the nation-building process, by the consolidation of a new model of economic development that perpetuated low levels of inter-societal and inter-state interdependence, and by the rise of the professional military as an autonomous political actor in the Southern Cone (Stepan 1973, 1978, 1988, Nunn 1976, Rouquié 1987) with a particular ideology to manage interstate relations. For most of the professional military, Geopolitics gradually came to provide "the theoretical foundations for the superior state leadership" (Von Chrismar 1968).

However, the late 19th century also experienced the stabilization of the inter-state system in the Southern Cone. One critical factor was the existence of an agreement, from the 1830s, on the common acceptance of the *uti possidetis* principle of 1810, whereby "the boundaries of the new states should coincide with those of the former Spanish administrative colonial divisions, sustaining their juridical basis". But the second factor was the material realities that the Triple Alliance War and the War of the Pacific introduced: the defeated countries had no alternative but to sign and legalize the new jurisdictional realities, which led to a new situation of what Kacowicz called "the territorial satisfaction with the status quo" of the main four powers, which was imposed on the smaller ones. In the Atlantic the status quo was cemented by the outcome of the Triple Alliance War. In the Pacific, it was fixed through a network of treaties between Chile and its rivals. With Argentina, relations were stabilized through the 1881 Treaty of Boundaries and the 1902 Pactos de Mayo. In relation to their common boundary, both countries agreed on the principle of *divisoria de aguas* [water divide], which defined the principle of the Atlantic for Argentina and Pacific for Chile while guaranteeing mutual access to both waters[21]. With Bolivia, Chile signed the 1904 Treaty of Peace, while stabilization with Peru came with the 1883 Treaty of Ancon and the 1929 Lima Protocols, which resolved the problem of the border provinces of Tacna and Arica.

According to Burr, if the first post-independence phase had structured two coastal sub-systems, the second phase cemented a continental system of balance of power based

---

[21] It is worth noting that both countries made enormous concessions in order to achieve the Treaty, but in doing so they consolidated their mutual perception as expansionist powers. Among other points, Chile renounced the immense Patagonian territory, while Argentina recognized Chilean sovereignty and rights on the Magellan Strait (Burr 1967: 154-5).

on the diagonal alliances of Argentina-(Bolivia)-Peru, and Brazil-Chile (Burr 1967:110-1, 260-3).

In short, the late 19th century was crucial for the Southern Cone. It basically defined the modern South American units and the systemic relationships that were to endure until the very late 20th century, thus also shaping their main strategic imperative and the consequent defense policies.

First, the above-mentioned territorial status quo emerged. Second, the territorial status quo was reached through a stable but precarious negative peace based on military domination and deterrence and on general agreements about the main issues under dispute. But many disputes remained unresolved. Chile and Argentina, as well as Chile and Peru, delayed several pending issues for further resolution, which meant that, despite the stability reached, unresolved issues could easily escalate into major conflicts if they were not properly managed, or if they were intentionally managed as diversionary wars[22], not to mention Bolivian dissatisfaction with the "status quo".

Third, the balance of power and territorial satisfaction with the status quo inhibited the use of force and prompted the development of alternative mechanisms of mediation and arbitration to settle disputes, actively used by Chile and Argentina after the War of the Pacific[23].

---

[22] During this period the classic example for crises that escalated toward diversionary wars before they were stopped was the 1920's Chilean mobilization on the northern border with Peru, also known as "La Guerra de Don Ladislao", a crisis mainly caused by domestic Chilean politics. See Meneses (1993: 370). The concept of diversionary war applies when "government provokes foreign conflict to rally the nation around the flag" (Barletta 2000: 154).

[23] Britain successively mediated and arbitrated after Argentina and Chile requested it during the execution of the 1881 Treaty of Boundaries and the 1902 Pactos de Mayo (Burr 1967: 248-560).

The international system favored this third feature in two senses. On the one hand, Britain encouraged the Chilean-Argentine recourse to mediation under the British Crown, aiming to keep its hegemonic position regarding the emerging power of the United States since the late 19th century (Burr 1967: 248-56, Kacowicz 1998: 94-6). On the other hand, Latin American countries were increasingly concerned by the imperial character of the U.S. policies toward the region, especially regarding its vocal (the Roosevelt Corollary) and factual behavior in the Caribbean Basin and, especially, in the Colombian (later Panamanian) isthmus. The weakening of Colombia was seen with concern by South American countries such as Chile, because it challenged its naval hegemony in the Southern Pacific and threatened the sub-system of balance of power that Santiago had carefully built mainly against Peru (Meneses 1989). In Argentina the Colombian issue was seen with concern because it favored the expansion and consolidation of Brazil. Thus, in the Southern Cone, after the territorial status quo, Argentine and Chilean fears of the United States' hegemonic ambitions through its Pan American projects (Kacowicz 1998: 95, Burr 1967, Meneses 1993: 402) prompted the first Argentine-Chilean cooperation, and even the first Chilean proposal for anti-U.S. coalition, the ABC Treaty between Argentina, Brazil, and Chile (Meneses 1989: 133)[24]. Although this initiative was formally explored but discarded by Brazil, it consolidated within the Southern Cone the

---

[24] The ABC Treaty was proposed by Chile in 1907 to Argentina and Brazil and again in 1914 in the context of the U.S. Pan American projects and intervention in Mexico, the Argentine-Chilean rapprochement after the 1902 Pactos de Mayo, and the end of the Argentine-Brazilian naval race at the beginning of World War I, and signed in 1915. It was proposed by Chile as a defensive alliance against an eventual U.S. aggression, but mainly as a Southern Cone arms (naval) control mechanism. Brazil was also partially interested because it feared that excessive U.S. support for Peru could weaken its then ongoing strategy of territorial consolidation in its Amazon perimeter. However, the Treaty was abandoned in 1917, when Brazil declared war on Germany and decided to follow the U.S. See Meneses (1989:132-9) and Pike (1963: 144-55).

principle of non-intervention among these three Southern Cone countries (Kacowicz 1998).

Thus, pacific settlement of disputes, mediation and arbitration, non-interference, in short an intense use of principles of international law, were also the outcome of the second period of the South American model of development after an initial period of intense use of inter-state physical force. They were maintained as the core of a South American cooperation regime that during the 20th century led to a long period of stability, which was interrupted only by the Chaco War and the Peruvian-Ecuadorian crises[25].

## C. THE ISI PERIOD: CONSOLIDATING AND EXACERBATING GEOPOLITICAL TENSIONS (1929-1983).

The liberal model of development fashioned by the region under British rule began to exhibit signs of exhaustion in some countries from the last years of the 19th century in its international, political, and societal dimensions. However, the real collapse of the Latin American export-led economic dependent model came with the international recession that began in 1929 and the rise of international protectionism, together with the demands for further democratization from the new, emerging middle classes and industrial workers. The outcome was a complete shift toward a different model of

---

[25] In fact, in the late 19th century Latin American countries began to champion the adoption of the principles of non-intervention and peaceful settlement of international disputes within the Pan American conferences persistently promoted by the Unites States. The Southern Cone countries were at the core of the movement. The Principle of Non-Intervention was adopted based on the legal doctrines elaborated by the Venezuelan/Chilean jurist Andres Bello and his *Principios del Derecho de Gentes* (1832), and later by the Argentine jurists Carlos Calvo and Luis M. Drago. The first resolution was approved in 1889 during the Washington Conference, and the U.S. voted against it. The second resolution was adopted in 1902 mainly as a Latin American response to U.S. interventions in the Caribbean Basin and two years before the Roosevelt Corollary. Finally, in the Seventh International Conference of American States held in Montevideo in 1933, the U.S. accepted a non-intervention treaty, although with reservations (Atkins 1995: 210-11, Burr 1967: 18).

economic development, but one that maintained high levels of political nationalism and low levels of economic interdependence among countries in the Southern Cone. As a result, the strategic rivalry and forms of cooperation shaped during the previous period remained unchanged.

### 1. International Framework.

Internationally, by the 1929 international economic crisis the U.S. had replaced Britain by a large margin as the main foreign economic actor and hegemonic power in Latin America, including the Southern Cone. However, during this period, this initial preeminence was heightened as the U.S. experienced its transformation toward world hegemonic power, a process that evolved between the two world wars.

The international system, upon which Southern Cone countries were highly dependent, also experienced deep transformations in its economic organization in two steps. First, it evolved from the liberal economic British order and the gold standard, to the Hamiltonian protectionist economic models developed against English domination by the United States and Germany (Gilpin 1987: 187-190, Keylor 1996: 3-127). Secondly, after World War II, the United States articulated global international economic regimes around the Bretton Wood institutions, regulating trade and investment within the sphere of influence it had negotiated with the Soviet Union during the late period of the war.

Regionally, Washington became the undisputed hegemon, reinvigorating the construction of a hegemonic hemispheric regime of collective security[26] through the Inter-American system. During this period the main goal of U.S. policies toward Latin America varied according to the international context. From 1929 to World War II it was

---

[26] For the concept of collective security see Kupchan and Kupchan 1995.

to align the region behind the U.S.-led coalition against German expansion, while during the Cold War Washington's relations with Latin America were subordinated to the strategy of containment in two phases. The first was organization of collective defense against a "foreign threat" (Germany and later the Soviet Union). The second focused on the containment of Latin American social and political movements, which were mostly qualified as "internal threats" fostered by a Soviet Union strategy to challenge the U.S. in the region, especially after the Cuban revolution in 1959, leading to a shift in U.S. policies in which the Inter-American system was reoriented from external defense toward the "internal" challenges, the so-called "national security" doctrines.

However, during the early 20th century U.S. relations with the Southern Cone regimes continued to be more complex than and very different from those with the rest of the Latin American countries. Argentina, Brazil, and Chile had greater power resources, were far from areas of vital interests, and exhibited higher levels of political autonomy.

Brazil exhibited a continuing preference for close alignment with the United States, which was perceived not only as economically useful for Brazilian development, but also helpful as a counterbalance against Argentine, Peru, Ecuador, Colombia, and France during the process of Brazilian territorial expansion and consolidation under the *uti possidetis* doctrine. Brazil perceived herself as an actor able to act "in condominium" with the United States regarding the hegemony of the Americas, that is, more as a partner than a subordinate, and the basic features of this policy were maintained during World War II and the Cold War[27].

---

[27] Smith notes that Brazil even expressed public support for the Monroe Doctrine and the Roosevelt Corollary (2000: 99).

Argentine grand strategy was similar in its aspirations but different in its alliances. Unlike the Brazilians, within a few years after Argentina's consolidation as a great South American power, Argentine leaders also began to envision themselves as the hegemonic power in South America[28], but opted for a closer relationship with declining Britain and became the most vocal champion of Latin American non-interventionism, openly directed against the United States (Smith 2000: 96-8). During the two world wars the outcome was a permanent neutrality but close proximity to European powers, and notably to the Axis during World War II, leading to the U.S. economic boycott between 1942 and 1949 (Escudé 1992: 237-78)[29]. Although Argentina finally shifted its position in 1945, it did so only under strong U.S. pressures (Escudé 1992: 257-76), and even after that, after the war, Buenos Aires tried to preserve its autonomy by initiating its military nuclear program during the Peronist regime. In the case of Chile, whose national power had abruptly declined in relation to Argentina's and Brazil's, the United States had to face the former country's trend toward neutrality, which was maintained until 1943 despite Washington's intense pressures. In that year Chile broke relations with the Axis -- only after the Nazi movement had become domestically tangible and closely associated with Peron's Argentine government--, and gradually began to embrace the Inter-American system (Varas *et Al.*1980: 85-101). By 1950, Chile was a full, if not the main, recipient of U.S. military aid in the Southern Cone (Joxe 197084-114)

---

[28] During the 1880s Argentine President Domingo Faustino Sarmiento publicly advocated an Argentine version of Manifest Destiny aimed at making the country a bioceanic power (Smith 2000: 97).

[29] Escudé notes that one of the reasons leading to the 1943 Argentine military coup was military concern about the strategic imbalances resulting from U.S. military assistance to neighbor countries (1992: 259).

Therefore, and despite important attempts to retain the highest levels of political sovereignty, the international system acted permanently as the basic context within which South American grand strategies and security strategies were framed politically, economically and strategically.

## 2. Domestic Framework. Political Nationalism, Economic Protectionism. and Continuing Low Interdependence.

From an economic perspective, for the Southern Cone countries, post-Depression alternatives were few[30]. The post-1929 world recession was accompanied by a wave of protectionism that began to be gradually and partially dismantled only under the U.S. hegemony after World War II. Therefore, when Latin American countries had to make their strategic economic decisions during the 1930s and 1940s, the international system was essentially protectionist, and this feature was maintained for several decades (Gilpin 1987: 180-84, Radelet and Sachs 1997). Domestically, the inward-looking strategy was reinforced by a combination of societal and institutional factors, among them the previous process of rapid urbanization under liberalization, which meant that when decisions were taken (even against sporadic attempts to reorient the economies toward an export-led pattern), urban political constituencies of import-substitution were stronger coalitions than the rural sector, which had declined in relative weight (Mahon 1992, Sachs 1985). The South American outcome was the development of the sub-regional version of protectionism, the import-substitution industrialization model (ISI), which endured until the 1980s debt crisis (Klarén 1986: 14-6, Cardoso and Helwege 1992: 73-137, Smith 1997: 52-62, Burns 1994: 226-59).

---

[30] We share Tomassini's assessment that "the strategy of import substitution was the only valid option open to them [the Latin American countries] at a given moment in their history, considering the stage of development that they had reached and the existence of an adverse external situation" (1985: 220).

The ISI model was essentially a variation of economic nationalism. With "high levels of effective protection and overvalued exchange rates" (Cardoso and Helwege 1992: 95), the outcome for Southern Cone inter-state relationships was the maintenance of the low levels of interdependence inherited from the past model. If during the 19th century transactions were essentially between each country and the capitalist metropolis, during the ISI period the pattern was maintained. Industrialization was local, but technology, imports, and capital came again from the capitalist core, especially from the United States, as shown in Figure 1 and Figure 2.

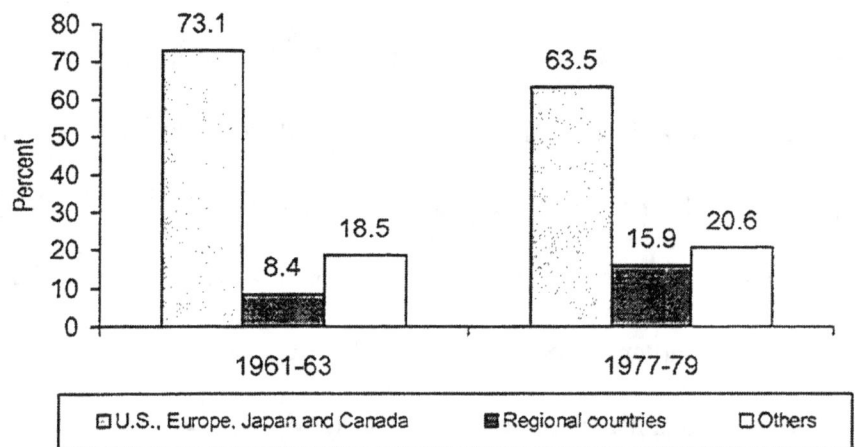

Figure 1. Destination of Latin American Exports.
*(Source: author, based upon Cardoso and Helwege 1999: 104)*

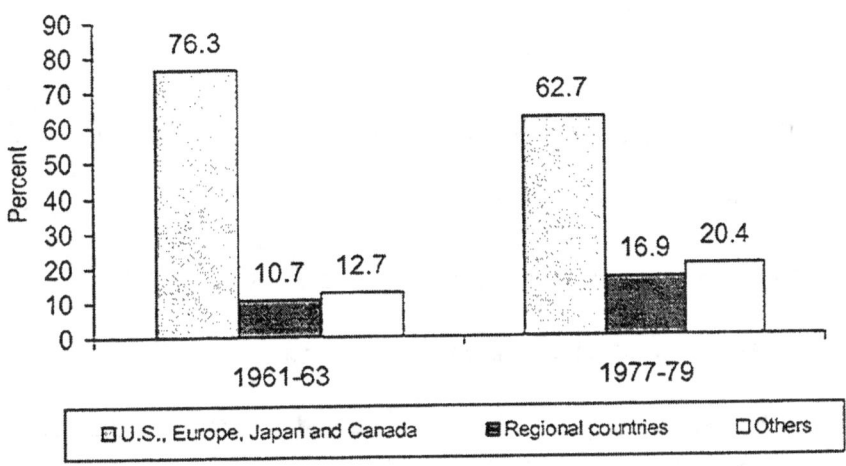

Figure 2. Origin of Latin American Imports.
*(Source: author, based upon Cardoso and Helwege 1999: 104)*

That the lack of interdependence was structural was tested and confirmed in the 1960s when the integrationist experiment was developed in Latin America within the ISI model, based on the European model of integration, and following the logic of seeking economies of scale. The policies failed because "the inherent contradiction between the idea of giving impetus to integration via trade liberalization and the protectionist logic of the import-substitution model did not provide a favorable context for integration" (Valls 1999: 8). The first experience was the Latin American Free Trade Zone (LAFTA) in 1960, followed in the Andean sub-region by the Andean Pact. Neither was able to solve the problems of "unbalanced gains from free trade" (Cardoso and Helwege 1999: 105).

In political terms the ISI model was initially associated with growing degrees of political democratization, because one of its main domestic objectives was to satisfy the growing demand for welfare and political participation raised by the emerging, largely urban middle and proletarian classes. Addressing the "social question" on the public agenda was an urgent task for progressive forces in all the countries, while industrial and agrarian bourgeoisies were often caught in contradictory postures. Thus, the economies were redesigned not only to accord with the real possibilities of the international markets, but also to face the rising social agenda imposed by rapid modernization. This led to an initial phase of more inclusionary[31] regimes that varied according to the specific dynamics of each country: democratic inclusion as in Chile until from 1931 to 1973, or authoritarianism as in Argentine or Brazilian populism or Peruvian military corporatism. However, in the end the ISI model produced structural and insurmountable balance-of-payment and fiscal deficits (Cardoso an Helwege 1992: 73-107) that left unresolved the growing social demands and led to authoritarian responses (O'Donnell 1986: 258,270). Because the model had been adopted in the entire region, it was a political crisis of regional dimensions, giving birth to the authoritarian regimes of the 1970s and the 1980s.

From a strategic perspective, the more significant consequence emanating from the domestic political regimes during the ISI period was the consolidation of the nationalist rationale within the political culture across the broad spectrum of political actors, encompassing civilian and military elites and masses. Nationalism was a natural result of inward-looking strategies of development.

### 3. Strategic Outcomes.

The Import-Substitution Industrialization period also consolidated an inter-state sub-system based on strategic rivalry and the extension of the 19th century balance of power. The core of the defense policies of the Southern Cone countries changed little from the 1865-70 Triple Alliance War against Paraguay, through the 1881 Argentine-Chilean and 1929 Chilean-Peruvian treaties, until 1985, the year of the Argentine-

---

[31] We use here the conceptualization proposed by Stepan (Stepan, 1978).

Brazilian rapprochement, except for its intensification. The maintenance of economic mutual isolation and low levels of interdependence played a key role in this process because there were no material incentives for cooperation and no economic institution for building trust. On the contrary, there were the inheritance and maintenance of numerous border or territorial disputes, and geopolitical distrust based on assumptions (right or wrong) about others' intentions.

For many scholars the strategic rivalry was increasingly exacerbated in direct proportion to the rise of the bureaucratic-authoritarian state (Child 1990), during which the state leadership of the complete sub-region gradually fell into the hands of true believers in and practitioners of geopolitics. This explanation has partial validity because there is a correlation between the growing prerogatives of the armed forces and incidence of military coups after World War II in Argentina, Brazil, and Chile (and the constitution of an authoritarian and militaristic self-fulfilling epistemic community of governing military dictators), and an increase in strategic rivalry[32], inter-state crisis, and arms build-up. Between 1974 and 1977, Bolivian and Peruvian military governments reactivated an aggressive campaign against Chile on the eve of the centennial anniversary of the War of the Pacific, causing a Chilean mobilization in its northern theater (Meneses 1993: 378). Also, in 1977-1978 Chile and Argentina experienced their worst bilateral crisis as a consequence of the Argentine rejection of the previously agreed British mediation in the Beagle Channel dispute. According to Escudé, the Argentine military regime "almost went to the war against Chile in the end of 1978, after having flagrantly violated

---

[32] Argentina began its nuclear program in 1950 during Domingo Peron's Presidency, creating the National Commission of Atomic Energy, igniting the Brazilian nuclear program in 1953. See Jones *et al* (1998).

international law by declaring *'nulo, de nulidad insanable'* the arbitral laud established by a previous arbitrating compromise signed in 1973" (1992: 41). Finally, the Argentine military junta launched the 1982 invasion of the Falklands/Malvinas Islands.

However, this explanation has only partial validity. It obscures the fact that when the process of democratization, liberalization, and integration began in the mid 1980s, the Southern Cone countries had strategic cultures forged in a long and gradual process of almost two centuries of lack of interdependence (and therefore few incentives for cooperation), border disputes, and geopolitical distrust, during which they had reached a "negative peace" (Kacowicz 1998: 9, 60).

Democratic Chile experienced several military crises between 1929 and 1973, most but not all of them with Argentina, long before the Chilean democratic breakdown. While the Brazilian-Argentine nuclear competition became critical after the 1982 Falklands/Malvinas War (Barletta 1999: 20-1), it had began long before, mostly as a result of the Argentine civil-military consensus for highly autonomous and expansionist foreign, defense and military policies, of which nuclear development after 1950 became a corollary (Escudé and Fontana 1998: 51-53, Jones, McDonough, Dalton and Koblents, 1998: 231).

In short, Southern Cone history created a strategic situation in which countries had the political will and developed the strategic capacities to militarily engage each other if necessary. It was a legitimate strategic rivalry deeply ingrained in both civilian and military elites, and in democratic or authoritarian regimes, based on objective and subjective past experience of geopolitical competition for resources and strategic positions, and cemented in a sub-regional balance of power that in the 20th century evolved toward a conflict management regime. Every country perceived the others as driven by an intrinsic expansionism in which economic reasons were a crucial originating force. Moreover, their economic development did not depend on the sub-region. Instead, it rested heavily on military deterrence against neighboring geopolitical threats.

As will be shown in the following chapter, during the late 1980s the international, political, and economic foundations that had generated the strategic ABC relationships during the 19th and 20th centuries were going to change. And with this, the strategic relationships were going to evolve toward conflict prevention regimes.

THIS PAGE INTENTIONALLY LEFT BLANK

# III. MODELS OF DEVELOPMENT AND INTERSTATE RELATIONS, 1983-2001: SUB REGIONAL COOPERATION, AND CONFLICT PREVENTION.

Given the outcome described and explained in Chapter II, it is striking to note that after an historical period that virtually encompassed all the countries' histories as independent states, their strategic relationships experienced a sudden, positive change toward improved cooperation in a period as short as a decade. The goal of this chapter is to describe and to explain this shift. We argue that the change in security cooperation was originated by the states' adoption of a new model of development informed by three interrelated variables--political democratization, economic liberalization, and sub-regional integration--whose causal roles varied during the process.

The changes in security cooperation were made within the critical context of the terminal crisis of the ISI economic model and/or on the exhaustion of the authoritarian regimes or both, which established clear priorities for the new governments. They needed to improve domestic political and/or economic conditions through a renovated and viable insertion in the changing international system.

From an economic point of view, the process by which the whole Latin American region shifted from the ISI model to the neo-liberal "Washington Consensus"[33] model was relatively long. First attempts were made during the 1960s with a series of intermittent initiatives toward structural adjustments[34]. However, the final push that

---

[33] The term "Washington Consensus" was coined by John Williamson to identify "10 areas where policymakers and scholars in 'Washington' could arguably muster a fairly wide consensus as to the character of the policy reforms that debtor countries should pursue" rights (1990: 9). The ten areas of policy reform were fiscal discipline, public expenditure priorities, tax reform, financial liberalization, exchange rates, trade liberalization, foreign debt investment, privatization, deregulation, and property.

[34] Previous, but failed, attempts at liberalization were made in Chile during the President Jorge

precipitated the entire transformation of the region into the neo-liberal model came from a the combination of several factors. Structural deficits accumulated by ISI became unsustainable under the succession of the oil crisis of 1974, the rise of U.S. interests rates, and the subsequent world recession of the early 80s. The outcome was the debt crisis (Cardoso and Helwege 1999: 116).

The crisis of the ISI model and the search for an economic alternative in the direction of market and export-oriented strategies had deeper consequences. First, it led to changes in political regimes. The last and declining period of the ISI model was managed by authoritarian regimes, and became an important factor eroding their legitimacy. This process was deeper in Argentina and Brazil, where the military regimes were unable to effect the economic reconversion. With different timing, it also happened in Chile, where the military government successfully began economic structural adjustment, but only after two painful recessions (in 1975 and 1983) that sparked widespread popular uprisings after 1983 and strengthened the heavily repressed Chilean opposition parties (Garretón 1989: 149-212). Between 1983 and 1990 the final outcome in the three countries was the crumbling of the authoritarian regimes, leading to the latest Latin American wave of democratization.

Second, the response to the ISI crisis meant changing the international insertion of each country, adapting strategies to the alternatives available within the international system led by the United States. In this sense, while regional change was essentially the

Alessandri government between 1958 and 1964, and by different administrations in Argentina in 1958-62, 1966-69, 1973-76, and 1978-81, and in Brazil in 1953-54, 1955-56, 1958-59, 1961, 1963, 1965-66, and 1991 (Skidmore and Smith 1997: 94-105, 128-30, 176-88; Cardoso and Helwege 1999: 99). In Peru, attempts were led by President Fernando Belaúnde during his second mandate (1980-85). See Sheahan (1999: 9).

consequence of domestic processes, it was reinforced by international factors following the end of the Cold War. Economically, if countries continued in the capitalist sphere, the Bretton Woods system offered a single option: structural adjustment as defined by the "Washington consensus". Alternative searches, like Alfonsín's non-alignment engagement strategy, were simply unviable[35]. In short, since ISI and socialism were exhausted, there were no available options except market liberalization and the variations within it. These ranged from extreme neo-liberalism (Williamson 1990), and the East Asian model (Sachs 1985), through the equity-growth model (Sheahan and Iglesias 1998) and second-generation reforms (Pastor and Wise 1999, Smith 2000), to a "third wave" approach more concerned with the erosion of the public sphere under neo-liberalism (Lechner 1998, Borón 1998).

Thus, democratization and liberalization were intertwined processes, although causal relationships between them are too complex to generalize, both being heavily strengthened by international dynamics (Remmer 1995, 1996). Also, since these processes began, democratic regimes in the region have tried to establish international regimes like the 1990s "Declaración de Santiago" (Farer 1986, Muñoz 2000) or the Democratic Clause of Mercosur (Milet, Fuentes and Rojas 1997: 37, Hirst 1999: 41) as part of a strategy aimed at overcoming trends toward democratic-deconsolidation (O'Donnell 1994, Diamond 1996).

However, and despite the complexity of the process, it is possible to identify different phases in which the causal roles of the variables have varied or have combined

---

[35] There is an extensive literature on the linkage among international global changes and the Latin America process of democratization. For the purposes of this paper we refer to Linz (1978: 18), Huntington 1991, Varas 1993, Rojas 1994, Remmer 1995, 1996, Diamond 1996, Milet, Fuentes and Rojas (1997: 16-28), Dominguez (1998: 3), and Smith (2000: 219-352).

to reinforce each other. The first step in security cooperation originated in the Argentine democratization in 1983, in which political calculations and ideological commitments played a causal role in ending strategic competition between Argentina and Brazil and establishing the first cooperative security regimes (Argentina and Chile). A second, also important process reinforcing the initial push from democratization emerged when economic factors began to act as an additional causal variable consolidating security cooperation; this resulted from the change from the ISI model to market liberalization, not only because of the exhaustion of the former model, but also because of the changes in the international system that left the countries with no alternatives for a viable insertion in the international system. The combination of both variables resulted in a strategic change in inter-state relationships.

## A. CHANGES IN POLITICAL REGIME TYPE AND SECURITY COOPERATION, 1983-1990.

Security cooperation between Argentina, Brazil, and Chile began to experience its main significant changes as a result of the process of political democratization that began in Argentina and was consolidated by the transitions to democracy in Brazil in 1985 and Chile in 1990.

Argentina was the first country able to end the authoritarian period in the Southern Cone, in 1983. Overwhelmed by a disastrous economic crisis, the defeat in the 1982 Malvinas/Falklands War, and increasing domestic contestation, the Argentine military regime returned the government to civilians, and President Raúl Alfonsín, leader of the *Unión Cívica Radical* party, assumed office in 1983 after winning the elections.

Alfonsín's initial tenure featured an extremely hostile environment, leading to the perception of a new democracy "under siege" both domestically and internationally[36]. Domestically, Alfonsín had to confront the legacies of the military regime, which involved not only managing the terminal crisis of the ISI Argentine model and the enormous external debt, but also addressing the problem of the massive human rights violations and the consequent possibility of an authoritarian regression. Internationally, the most immediate concerns of the new Argentine democratic government was its isolation within the Southern Cone, where it was surrounded by military regimes that were presumed by Alfonsín's administration to be hostile both to the Argentine state and to its fragile democracy. The result was the articulation of an Argentine foreign policy that radically attempted to stabilize the strategic Southern Cone environment aiming to dissipate external sources of domestic instability. In chronological order, the main efforts were directed at Chile and Brazil.

1. **Argentine-Chilean Security Cooperation Since 1983. The Politics of Democratization and Democratic Consolidation.**

   *a. Security Cooperation Between Alfonsín's Democratic and Pinochet's Authoritarian Regime.*

During the initial period, the first significant policy that Alfonsín's foreign policy team, led by Foreign Minister Dante Caputo, successfully developed was the settlement of the most pressing border disputes Argentina had had pending with Chile since the 19th century, and which had led both countries to the brink of war during the 1978 crisis, the Beagle Channel dispute, in which both countries had contending visions of their jurisdiction over the waters of the channel and three adjacent islands (Picton,

---

[36] For a detailed analysis of this period of the Argentine dynamic see Fournier (1999), Barletta (1998).

Nueva, and Lennox) strategically located in the connection between the Atlantic and the Pacific oceans, whose possession had important and strategic projections regarding the access of each country to the oceans, the Economic Exclusive Zone (EEZ) resources, and their claims over the Antarctic. In 1983, when President Alfonsín assumed the government both countries were still in a military crisis situation and fully mobilized. War had been avoided at the last minute in 1978 because of the combined effect of the Chilean deterrence and the intervention of the Pope John Paul II, whose mediation was accepted by both military regimes (Meneses 1993: 378, Pion-Berlin 2000). However, the problem had not been resolved because the Argentine government had rejected not only the British judgment in 1977, which favored Chile, but also resisted the Vatican posture, which also tended to favor Chile. The possibility of a new military escalation was, therefore, real if the crisis was not properly managed.

Alfonsín's solution was simple. It radically innovated in the Argentine position by accepting the Papal judgment, which was, like the 1977 British Arbitral Laud, "substantially in favor of Chile" (Schmitter 1991: 106); signing the bilateral Treaty of Friendship and Cooperation in 1984; and submitting the Treaty to plebiscitarian ratification in May 1985.

The Treaty had major effects on Argentine-Chilean strategic relationships. It not only definitely solved the dispute in the austral zone, but also established procedures to solve future territorial disputes between the parties. It reduced also the level of mutual threat perception, leading to a sustained process of demilitarization and demobilization even under Pinochet's regime. Furthermore, it reinforced the sectors in both countries supporting the recourse to regimes of pacific settlement of disputes, continuing the Southern Cone's historical tradition, and created the conditions for the first time in the countries' bilateral history to develop new forms of security cooperation aimed at conflict prevention and not only the management of already-erupted crises. Both consequences of the 1984 Treaty were important because although the Treaty diminished the Argentine-Chilean strategic rivalry, it did not end it. Even after its signature, the two countries still had 24 other border disputes, which continually regenerated mutual distrust.

In terms of security cooperation the main innovation introduced by the Treaty was the adoption of the first set of Confidence Building Measures (CBM)[37], which aimed to avoid the emergence of unintended crises in the former zone of dispute, but also to improve military-to-military communications. The first measures were developed after 1986 between the naval and air forces of both countries, and were later extended to their armies and even to their police forces (Caro 1994: 195).

### b. Security Cooperation Between Democratic Regimes: the Menem and Aylwin Administrations.

If Argentine democratization was able to spark security cooperation with authoritarian Chile during the 1980s, the end of the Alfonsín's administration in 1990 became an important moment regarding its continuity because in that year there were changes not only of government in Argentina but also of regime in Chile, when Carlos

---

[37] Most restricted concepts of Confidence Building Measures (CBM) define them as "agreements of cooperation through which states transmit their non-hostile military intentions". However, it is worth noting that the debate about the concept of CBM accepts other wider definitions of CBMs. For instance, Krepon and Varas describe them as "steps to improve existing political relations and, through this way, reduce the probability of a war". This definition could include a wide variety of measures, such as those addressing border or trade disputes, but they "must have a direct impact in obtaining a more stable peace" (Krepon and Varas 1994: 10-11).

Menem and Patricio Aylwin assumed the presidencies of Argentina and Chile, respectively.

Both changes had a positive impact. Cooperation was maintained and even increased despite the fact that Chile was not participating in the economic integration process launched by Argentina and Brazil in 1986 and by these two countries plus Paraguay and Uruguay around Mercosur in 1991. On the Argentine side, Menem's administration imprinted a radical change on Argentine foreign policy but maintained full continuity with Alfonsín's bilateral relations with Chile (Escudé 1992: 32-3, 36). In the Chilean case, Aylwin's administration maintained a high degree of continuity in Chilean bilateral policies regarding Argentina, but evidenced a clear political will to advance toward improved relationships, putting a clearer, stronger stress on security cooperation with Argentina than Pinochet's regime had done, and--as Alfonsín had done during his tenure--adopting radical steps toward bilateral detente, security cooperation and integration in other areas. The new, democratically elected President in Chile gave "central priority" to bilateral relations with neighboring countries, focusing the relationships on the consolidation of security issues, a focus that was favored and encouraged by the positive disposition of the Argentine and Brazilian governments. According to Van Klaveren, Chilean political authorities began "to speak of the new 'neighborhood policy', precisely to describe a policy that aimed toward the overcoming of old border issues, with respect to the traditional [Chilean] principles, and that pretended to provide a new framework for growing interdependent relationships with the natural Chilean environment" (Van Klaveren 1997: 128, Insulza 1998).

As Fournier has shown, democratic leaders and parties in both countries had realized the importance of security cooperation for their processes of democratic transition and consolidation, and their political collaboration had began even before 1990[38]. Thus, in 1990 both the Argentine and Chilean governments were converging toward a general improvement in their bilateral relationship, a political climate that allowed further advances during the first year of both newly elected governments.

The first move toward security cooperation was in April 1991, when both governments agreed to institutionalize annual meetings between Joint Military Staffs. It led to the expansion and consolidation of the CBMs, including joint naval exercises in the Beagle Channel, aerial exercises, and military institutional interchanges, for the first time in their bilateral history (Caro 1994: 195, Cheyre 2000: 69).

However, the second and most important advance was registered in August 1991, when Presidents Menem and Aylwin signed their first Joint Argentine-Chilean Presidential Declaration, containing a broad spectrum of agreements ranging from resolution of crucial border disputes to initial steps toward integration. Among the declaration's main points, the presidents supported the agreements previously reached by the Joint Border Commission created by the 1984 Treaty and agreed on solutions to 22 of the 24 border disputes that were pending after the 1984 Treaty. Menem and Aylwin also agreed on the basic principle of seeking negotiated solutions for the two most important and contentious issues: the border in the Campo de Hielos and Laguna del Desierto. The

---

[38] Dominique Fournier makes an important point by noting that a few months before Alfonsín's inauguration the Argentine and Chilean democratic opposition jointly met and requested their respective military governments to reopen negotiations on the Beagle Channel. "It is clear from the August 1983 joint statement that they linked this foreign policy initiative with the strengthening of eventual democratization processes in their respective countries" (Fournier 1999: 64, fn. 106).

former would take the rest of the decade to resolve, while the latter would be submitted to an arbitrated solution, which was dictated in 1994 in favor of the Argentine position. After exhausting the procedures jointly established for appeal, Chile finally accepted the arbitral decision and ratified the judgment (Caro 1994: 195-6, Cheyre 2000: 32). Finally, the 1991 Joint Presidential Declaration also established the basis for cooperation regarding bilateral integration and the "creation of a free trade zone by 1995", encompassing economic, scientific, administrative, financial, naval, energy, telecommunications, tourism and educational sectors, among other areas. Particularly important was the beginning the cooperation on mining and energy, aiming at energy interconnection and a Treaty of Mining Integration (Varas and Fuentes 1994: 200-2).

Finally, in 1994 the Argentine-Chilean rapprochement began to exhibit a clear, second stage of security cooperation at higher levels, which was motivated by an accelerating increase in levels of economic interdependence between 1990 and 1994. During this second period calculations on political stability and ideological commitment between democratic parties continued to play an important role. In 1996 Mercosur incorporated the democratic clause in its foundational Treaty, which was also accepted by Chile and Bolivia the same year, establishing the incompatibility between integration and political association, on the one hand, and non-democratic regimes, on the other (Guilhon 1999: 272).

## 2. The political Origins of the Argentine-Brazilian Security Cooperation.

If the Argentine-Chilean rapprochement initiated in 1984 was a turning point in this bilateral relationship, Alfonsín's government policies regarding cooperation with

Brazil were even more radical and visible after the 1985 transition to democracy in that country and the election of José Sarney as Brazilian President.

Animated by the same Kantian foreign policy ideologies and political calculations that guided his policy toward Chile, Alfonsín persuaded his Brazilian counterpart (Barletta 1999: 25) to join in developing of a process of cooperation focused on nuclear cooperation and economic integration, with the explicit political purpose of reducing military interference in their respective domestic processes of democratic consolidation and strengthening their respective domestic political positions[39].

Although bilateral cooperation had been advanced during the military governments, the steps adopted by Alfonsín and Sarney were far more radical, for the development of nuclear weapons in both countries was externally seen as highly probable after the strategic assessments of the role performed by nuclear technologies during the Malvinas/Falklands war (Barletta 1999). The governments aimed not only to reduce the possibility of conflict between two long-standing rivals through CBMs (as in the Argentine-Chilean case during the 1980s), but also to suppress the possibility of a conflict by ending the military character that both programs had developed and launching a process of economic integration (Barletta 1999: 23-6, Diamint 1999: 51, Fournier 1999: 46). In November 1985 Argentina and Brazil signed the Foz de Iguazú Declaration, committing them to develop nuclear power for peaceful uses only; in 1986, both countries signed the bilateral Treaty of Integration, Cooperation and Development, beginning formal security cooperation in the aeronautical and nuclear sectors. The former

---

[39] Scholars tend to agree that Sarney's motivations to accept Alfonsín's initiative were similar, but the process that conduced to his decision was more complex because of the Brazilian foreign policy making process. See Schmitter 1991, Hirst 1996, Soares 1996, 1999, Barletta 1999.

was developed through potent symbolic gestures such as Presidential visits to previously secret atomic plants at Picalniyeu (Argentina) and Aramar (Brazil) in 1988 and the development of a sophisticated network of bilateral CBMs in the nuclear field. The latter was deepened by the 1990 Protocolo de Buenos Aires, and the creation of Mercosur on May 26, 1991 with the Treaty of Asunción (Hirst 1998: 103, Guilhon 1999: 263-4, Pion-Berlin 2000: 45-6, Hirst 1999: 36).

### 3. Multilateral Security Cooperation.

It is also important to underline that the bilateral rapprochements first between Argentina and Chile, but especially between Argentina and Brazil, produced a clear improvement of the regional security environment, which in turn, together with other international factors such as the intense U.S. pressures against weapons of mass destruction in the Third World[40], favored the development or consolidation of several security regimes during the 1990s.

First, the Argentine-Brazilian nuclear strategic rapprochement strengthened the Southern Cone's participation in non-proliferation regimes. Both countries entered and ratified the Non Proliferation Treaty (NPT), the Tlatelolco Treaty, the Comprehensive Test Ban Treaty (CTBT), and the Missile Technology Control Regime (MTCR), among others (Jones *et al* 1998). Despite being a non-nuclear state, until the 1990s Chile had not ratified the NPT, but did so only in 1995, after Argentina. Also, in 1991 Argentina, Brazil, and Chile (and later Uruguay) signed the Mendoza Compromise, through which the Southern Cone countries agreed not to produce, develop, stockpile, or transfer

---

[40] U.S. concerns were related not only to the eventual development of strategic capabilities (nuclear weapons and delivery technologies) in Brazil and Argentina, but also, the eventual transference of this technology to the Middle East. See Fitch (1994: 86-7).

chemical weapons, and in 1993 those countries together with several other Latin American states also signed the United Nations Convention on Chemical Weapons. Because Argentina, Brazil, and Chile were signatories of the U.N. Convention on Biological Weapons, a secondary effect of the strategic rapprochements in the Southern Cone was, therefore, the agreement on arms control regimes that consolidated Latin America as the only continent free of weapons of mass destruction.

Finally, changes in political regimes strengthened other regimes linked to regional security. In 1990 Chile entered the Rio Group, the main Latin American political mechanism of political concertation and alternative forum to the U.S.-dominated OAS (Frohman 1990)[41], where political and security issues are intensively discussed between states (Van Klaveren 1997: 133). In June 1991 Chile played a pivotal role in prompting the adoption of the Santiago Declaration (Resolution AAG/RES 1080) of the Organization of American States (OAS), which instituted a democratic clause in the charter of the continental institution (Farer 1996).

Therefore, and contrary to other experiences in which democratization may increase the "danger of war" (Mansfield and Snyder 1995), the politics of democratization in the Southern Cone--that is, the quest to consolidate the new democratic regimes in Argentina, Brazil, and Chile--and democratic ideological factors were necessary conditions for security cooperation. However, it would be wrong to conclude that democratization was sufficient to sustain security cooperation in the long term. Schmitter acknowledged this in 1991 pointing out that:

---

[41] The Rio group also includes Mexico, the Central American Common Market, the G-3 and the Andean Community. However, the Mexican influence in Latin American affairs has declined since its incorporation to NAFTA, which restricted its economic room of maneuver, which in turn has increased the relative weigh of Brazil and Mercosur.

The lessons from the *Cono Sur* are encouraging from a neoidealist perspective, but they are not conclusive. The transition from authoritarian to democratic rule had made a significant difference in inter-state relations within the subregion, but it would certainly be premature to draw the conclusion that 'permanent cooperation' or 'permanent peace' has been attained (...). All we can say certainly is that the demise of despotic government has produced a significant decline in the likelihood of recourse to interstate violence and an unprecedented increase in the volume of interstate agreement. However, the citizens of these countries have yet to generate a volume and variety of mutual trade, investment, production, tourism, labor flows, and social communications sufficient to modify their much more important and persistent dependence upon extraregional partners (Schmitter 1991: 119).

Domestic legitimacy of integration may begin as elite-sponsored, but to become sustainable in the long term after the governing elites that initiated the process are gone, it must continue to be supported by a substantive, hegemonic coalition of societal or political forces[42]. This feature--the endurance and deepening of the process-- is also a key element in its articulation with security and defense policies, because the latter usually responds to long-term trends and involve cycles of strategic planning that are necessarily long because of the amount of public resources committed to them, and the length of life-cycle of weapons systems (Meneses and Navarro 1989). In this sense, the change of the economic model toward liberalization and integration of the intra-regional markets was a substantial step toward a deeper sub-regional rapprochement not only between Argentina and Brazil, but among all of the countries, ameliorating mutual traditional threat perceptions and stimulating security and military cooperation far beyond the exclusive nuclear field initially promoted by Alfonsín and Sarney.

---

[42] For other studies about the difficulties of generalizing causal relationship between domestic political regimen and foreign policy in the Southern Cone case see Van Klaveren (1996: 43-5).

Therefore, the study of the economic relationships after the initial period of democratization seems necessary, and it will be developed in the second part of this chapter.

## B. DEMOCRATIC CONSOLIDATION THROUGH ECONOMIC LIBERALIZATION AND ECONOMIC INTEGRATION.

After the initial period of democratization, Argentina and Brazil converged with Chile in adopting market economies, thus consolidating the initial impetus toward economic integration. As also happened during the first phase, economic reforms and integration were governed in each country by its government's political calculations aiming to maintain and consolidate its political stability and democratic regime. However, the change of economic models and the rise of deep economic interdependence increased the demand for more intensive and extensive conflict prevention regimes, shifting security cooperation toward a more advanced phase, in which past perception of the "other" as a rival or even as an enemy was replaced by perception of him as a necessary partner to consolidate domestic welfare. In the end, from simple forms of conflict prevention, countries advanced toward genuine forms of cooperative security. Therefore, increasing interdependence resulting from the integration process and domestic processes of market liberalization also acted as an intervening variable originating security cooperation.

To address this formulation, the following two subsections will explain the political rationale behind the processes of economic liberalization and integration in Argentina, Brazil, and Chile. The third will describe the changes in economic interdependence. The fourth will explain how the new economic models changed the strategic relationships between the countries and how this new context improved their security cooperation.

### 1. Political Contexts of Argentine-Brazilian Economic Reform and Integration.

If during the first phase (1983-1990) the strategic rapprochement between Argentina and Brazil was driven by domestic political calculations and ideological reasons in both countries, there is a clearly identifiable a second phase when the respective military establishments ceased to be the main source of instability for the new democratic regimes, and the main problems for democratic stability and consolidation became the poor economic performance of the governments during the mandate of presidents Alfonsín and Sarney. Domestic and foreign policies were adjusted to serve this new priority of the Argentine and Brazilian democracies and became--in this sense-- economically driven. Ultimately, increased economic interdependence would introduce new demands and additional rationales for increased security cooperation.

Therefore, between the 1980s and 1990s the Argentine-Brazilian process of integration experienced a shift in its rationale, from one centered on the challenges to democratic consolidation posed by the military (and built upon strategic nuclear cooperation), to another in which economic survival and economic performance became the primary test for democratic consolidation.

In the case of Argentina, economic integration became a crucial condition for its successful re-insertion in the international economy after a half century of free rider and anti-American power politics. Despite Alfonsín's notable achievements in improving the sub-regional strategic environment, the Radical President was overwhelmed by his incapacity to manage the economy and, humiliated, resigned months before the scheduled date. President Carlos Menem assumed office in 1990 and inherited a country suffering from an economic crisis featuring hyperinflation and from political instability arising from human-rights judicial processes against the former military leaders. The new government shifted the agenda axis from one centered on civil-military relations to another whose *leit motiv* was the imperative of economic recovery, which also became the main goal of Menem's foreign and security policies[43]. Despite his *Justicialista* political origins, which had made expectable a strong commitment to the state-centered policies of Perón (or maybe exactly because of the opportunistic nature of Peronist populism), the new administration realized that it faced a "terminal crisis of autarkic capitalism" (Waisman 1999: 105) and that economic international insertion in the 90s implied market liberalization and structural adjustment.

The integrationist project acquired new impetus within this new framework. Argentine leaders rapidly opened and deregulated the economy and reintroduced an export-led model. However, another strategic decision was made. The Argentine economy would be opened through a two-phased strategy. The first would be the process of sub-regional economic integration, already sketched in the 1986 Argentine-Brazilian Treaty, which could foster economic recovery through the penetration of the huge Brazilian economy. Second the integration process would be a necessary transition toward a gradual, long-term, more complete opening to the external economy, and in the meantime the Argentine economy would become more competitive (Skidmore and Smith 1997: 110-13). The strategy was adopted and in its first years was clearly successful.

---

[43] Because the Argentina's particular civil-military balance of power, Menem was able to definitely solve the problem of civilian control of the military early in his tenure. His firm control of the military became evident during the 1990 *carapintada* uprising which was bloodily crushed (Linz and Stepan 1996: 190-204, Hunter 1996, 1997, Waisman 1999: 101)

Exports increased over 50 percent from 1990 to 1995, but Mercosur became the key: in 1996 Argentine export to the group rose to 33 percent of its total (Waisman 1999: 100).

Brazil presented a different context, but the sequence was essentially the same. Five years after its inauguration the main problem for the democratic regime was the erosion of its legitimacy resulting from its high levels of corruption, poor economic performance, and lack of efficacy and efficiency. In 1989 "citizens believed that the situation was better under the military regime of 1964-85 than under the first four years of civilian democratic rule" (Linz and Stepan 1996: 173, 180). The Brazilian military did not present an immediate and direct threat to the democratic regime's survival. Nevertheless, the military were in a stronger position than in Argentina. They had retained institutional prerogatives, and their contestation was open and more politically articulated, so they were a serious political alternative to the new Brazilian democratic government should it be unable to address the country's problems (Hunter 1997, Agüero 2000: 85-87). Thus, with Brazil facing an new imminent regime crisis economics also became the key rationale for the integration process, which was crucial to improve the economic performance of the government and, in turn, advance toward higher levels of democratic consolidation. From a technical point of view many Brazilian leaders realized that they needed to transform the big but highly subsidized and protected Brazilian economy, and especially its industrial sector, to a more efficient and internationally competitive one. But at the same time they were also conscious that it would require a strategy whose pace would be as fast as the domestic political conditions of a democratic regime would permit. Thus, Brazilian elites converged with Argentina's. Integration could be a more tolerable strategy of liberalization than the simple but politically costly "Washington Consensus".

Therefore, a few years after the Argentine-Brazilian strategic rapprochement had began for political reasons, by the 1990s this rapprochement had maintained its strategic character, but it had also been enhanced. The economic integration became economically strategic for the success of economic reform and democratic stability in both countries. Economic integration was to be continued, but it needed to be reformulated to become coherent with two increasingly market- and export-oriented economic models that were also interested in maintaining or even increasing their diversification. The crucial point was how to make regional integration compatible with a diversified export structure coherent with the evolution of the General Agreement on Tariffs and Trade (GATT), later the World Trade Organization (WTO)[44]. The solution adopted was a moderate and limited version of the "Open Regionalism" strategy, in which regional integration is conceived as complementary, not antithetical, to liberalization. To this purpose, countries create a customs union, but also commit to continuously downgrade their barriers to economic factors, and to apply the Most Favored Nation GATT principle to third countries (like Chile) or even regions (like the European Union) that reciprocate[45].

---

[44] In this context, the contrast between the 1986 type of integration and that of the Treaty of Asuncion, which established Mercosur in May 1991, is evident. While the Argentine-Brazilian 1986 Program for Integration and Economic Cooperation (PICE) focused on promoting industrial exports and regulating trade balances, and was therefore still linked to the ISI model (Valls 1999: 9), the Treaty of Asunción scheduled a timetable for gradually establishing a free trade area, a customs union, and a common market, but also made a formal commitment to gradually expand the benefits to third countries.

[45] The Latin American concept of Open Regionalism was coined by ECLAC (1994, 1999: 21). See also Urriola and Rebolledo (1998: 180). However, Van Klaveren correctly notes that Open Regionalism antedates the ECLAC 1994 definition. It was adopted by the Asia Pacific Economic Cooperation (APEC) in 1989 and Mols attributes the original concept to Chong Li Choy in 1981 (Mols 1996: 19). Also, Fred Bergsten, the former president of the APEC's Eminent Persons Group, and director of the Institute for International Economics, distinguishes between five different concepts of Open Regionalism and considers

Thus, and following traditional theories of economic integration[46], the Argentine and Brazilian governments (together with Paraguay and Uruguay) finally agreed on the creation of Mercosur through the Treaty of Asunción, signed on March 26, 1991 by the head of state of Argentina, Brazil, Paraguay and Uruguay. It entailed three main economic goals: the creation of a free trade area; the establishment of a customs union; and the coordination of macroeconomic policies, as well as the harmonization of domestic legislation in sectors relevant to integration. Later, the 1994 Treaty of Ouro Preto granted Mercosur an international juridical personality under international law.

The Treaty of Asunción also created an intergovernmental institutional structure, which was updated in 1994 by the Treaty of Ouro Preto: First, decision-making was assigned to the Council of the Common Market, comprising the Presidents, and ministers of foreign affairs and economy. The Council can also call other ministers. Mercosur also created the Forum for Consultations and Political Concertation, which included integrated by high officials representing each country. Second, executive faculties were granted to the Group of the Common Market, composed of high officials representing

---

that Mercosur does not fit within any of them (Bergsten 1997: 550).

[46] Traditional theories of economic integration argue that liberalization within a region of several states favors economies of scale and reduces transaction costs of economic goods, leading to a more efficient resource allocation. Thus, regional markets are created through a linear process involving the establishment of a free trade area, followed by a customs union, a common market, economic union, and, finally, by total economic integration. The creation of regional markets makes it necessary to clear market distortions originated by different national regulations, and integration creates a demand for coordination of macroeconomic policies and the consequent self-restriction in some degree of sovereign economic decision making. See Balassa (1961), Nye (1971), and for recent economic reassessment see Lindert and Pugel (1996: 201-222), Budnevich and Zahler (1999). The Inter-American Development Bank notes that between Latin American economists there are two contending schools of thought: the *monetary approach*, which argues for a single currency at this early stage of the integration process, and the *structural approach*, which argues that an "optimal currency area" can only be created in the end of the integration, after a long process of macroeconomic coordination and convergence. This latter approach, closer to European strategies of economic integration, "appears to have gained ground within Mercosur" (IADB 1999).

each country, and, later, to the Mercosur's Trade Commission. Also, Mercosur established also a Joint Parliamentary Commission integrated by members of national parliaments, an economic and social Consultative Forum, and an administrative secretariat, but their roles are still secondary.

## 2. Political Context of Chilean Economic Reform, and Integration.

Chile's process toward economic, political, and physical integration with the sub-region presents several commonalties but also differences compared with those of Argentina and Brazil. The Chilean economic liberalization began in the mid-70s and was fully applied by 1984, long before the 1990 transition to democracy (Garretón 1989, Haggard and Kaufman 1995:76: 76-83), that is, six years before Argentina and eleven before Brazil. Therefore, during its first phase, the transformation from ISI to market-oriented economy was led by Pinochet's regime, authoritarian and politically isolated, implementing a model heavily dependent on foreign investment and the success of the export strategy. Tariffs were unilaterally lowered and in 1990 were at 11% as a strategy to foster and diversify export markets. As a result, when the new democratic regime led by Patricio Aylwin began its tenure in 1990, and while Argentina and Brazil were beginning their respective processes of liberalization and economic integration, Chile was fully liberalized in comparative terms and oriented toward a diversified export-led strategy, as shown in Figure 3.

This context led to a cautious response from Chile in 1993 when Brazilian President Itamar Franco, during a Rio Group Summit in Santiago, invited Chile and other countries to join Mercosur and to create a South American Free Trade Area (Leite Ribeiro 1997: 54). On the one hand, as previously seen, Chilean democratic political leaders were strong supporters of increasing security cooperation, and because of Chile's more advanced market deregulation, Chilean firms were in better condition to compete in a process of regional market liberalization. Thus, there were both ideological, political, security, and economic incentives for a favorable Chilean policy toward Mercosur. However, on the other hand, and despite its favorable and explicit predisposition toward sub-regional cooperation, the more liberalized stage of the Chilean economy imposed a high barrier to Chile's integration in Mercosur, forcing the Aylwin administration to moderate its initial impetus regarding economic integration. The main problem was that integration would have forced Chile to raise its tariffs to enter the customs unions of a market like Mercosur[47], which in 1990 represented only the eight percent of its exports, while reducing its competitiveness in all the others (Saavedra-Rivano 1996: 101, Van Klaveren 1997: 125). It would have been, therefore, a major departure from an economic model that had been successful for the Chilean economy[48], but without clear economic advantages.

Also, during the first democratic period Chilean authorities were divided between those who preferred to underline the "exceptional" character of the Chilean economy within the sub-region and to adopt an isolationist strategy regarding Latin America, and those who stressed the strategic importance of the integration process and the growing economic relevance the region was assuming for Chile. While the former were clearly more interested in the Chilean accession to the North American Free Trade Agreement (NAFTA), the latter saw economic, political, and strategic opportunities in Mercosur (Van Klaveren 1997, Insulza 1998).

However, four factors shifted the Chilean positions when the second democratic government took office. First, the debate was partially resolved when the U.S. Congress in 1994 denied to U.S. President Bill Clinton the fast track authority to negotiate the Chilean accession to NAFTA. Second, Chile's economic stake in Mercosur countries was growing. The Chilean private sector had *de facto* began to penetrate the group's countries through both finance and trade. After ten years of privatization of pensions that raised the national saving rates to levels up to 20 percent, Chile became a capital exporter and

---

[47] In 1991 the Chilean average tariff was 10.5 percent, while the Argentine was 14.2 and the Brazilian 20.4 percent. See Devlin *et al* 1999, IADB 2000.

[48] Between 1983-1989 the average Chilean GDP growth was 5.2 percent, and 7.7 between 1990-1993. Between 1994-1999 it was 5.7 percent. See Le Fort (2000: 8).

needed financial markets. Meanwhile, Latin America and Mercosur became the most promising market for the Chilean industrial and service sectors, making it more profitable than Europe, Japan and North America, where exports were limited to raw materials (Saavedra-Rivano 1996: 103, Robledo 1997: 190-8, Milet 1998: 35, Van Klaveren 1997: 127), and the Chilean government and the private sector organizations were conscious that once the customs union began, the better option for non-Mercosur countries would be to negotiate an agreement (Insulza 1998: 79). Third, the Chilean foreign policy elite was highly aware that the integration process within the Southern Cone meant "the redesign of the geopolitical scenarios that have predominated during the 20th century" and the rise of an unprecedented South American international actor. According to Frei's Foreign Affairs Minister, "it is emerging in our borders a new unified market and a new political reality with strong international projections" (Insulza 1998: 79)[49]. And fourth, the Chilean government was highly stimulated, like their liberal counterparts in Argentina and Brazil, by the role Mercosur could perform in promoting democratic stabilization[50]. A positive impact of Mercosur on the Chilean economy was seen as a factor strengthening the social and political legitimacy of the ruling democratic coalition after 1990, featured by a successful economic performance, which has been crucial for its long endurance from 1990 to date (Linz and Stepan 1996: 225, Valenzuela 1999: 240).

[49] José Miguel Insulza became a highly influential Chilean political figure during the late 1990s. He was Foreign Affairs Minister from 1994 to 1999, when he was nominated Minister of Interior, the second political and protocolar position in the Chilean executive, because his tenant must replace the President in case of absence or vacancy. After the 1999 elections and the arrival of President Ricardo Lagos's administration in 2000, Insulza was confirmed as Minister of Interior.

[50] Despite little research has been done in this area, it is clear that the democratic Chilean officials that assumed the government in 1990 were part of what could be called an epistemic community of believers in the merits of integrationist policies. For instance, see José Miguel Insulza, Chilean Foreign Minister between 1995-2000 (Somavía and Insulza 1990, Insulza 1998a, 1998b).

Ultimately, the Frei Administration decided to shift the Chilean foreign policy toward Mercosur by adopting an intermediate option between non-integration and the customs union. It assumed Mercosur was a "strategic option" (Insulza 1998: 77), but proposed to negotiate an association treaty, which was signed in San Luis de Mendoza on June 25, 1996, after Mercosur accepted Chilean conditions. The Treaty was three-pillared:

First, it was a free trade agreement between Mercosur and Chile compatible with the GATT/WTO rules. It contemplates an eight-year program of tariff reduction, and three special lists for sensitive products (3, 10, and 10 to 15 years of exemptions), and includes progressive liberalization of services and trade, mechanisms for disputes solution after 2000. Second, it contained a protocol of physical integration based on the construction of twelve inter-oceanic corridors to connect the Platine Basin with Chilean sea-ports to transport goods to and from the Asia-Pacific region across Chilean-Argentine-Brazilian territory; sea-ports were seen with enormous interest by Argentina and Brazil, and as a key component of the Chilean "strategic goal of becoming a bridge between the Atlantic and the Pacific" (Van Klaveren 1997: 130). Chile and Argentina also established gas pipelines and electric interconnections to supply the growing Chilean demand with Argentine energy, and negotiated a mining protocol to exploit mineral resources through joint ventures along the *cordillera* border, which in 2001 was awaiting Congressional ratification. Last, but not least, the Chile-Mercosur Treaty was expanded to include incorporation of Chile in Mercosur's political intergovernmental decision making institutions (except for the customs union).

Thus, Chile entered the economic integration process five years after Mercosur's beginning[51], but it was Argentina and Brazil who continued to liberalize their markets, while Chile deepened its economic strategy and did not raise its tariffs. Indeed, Chile continued its policy of multiple economic insertion through several new bilateral and multilateral agreements, entering the Asia-Pacific Economic Cooperation in 1994 and signing a cooperation agreement with the European Union aimed at a free trade zone only two days before signing with Mercosur (Saavedra-Rivano 1996: 101). Finally, in September 2000, the U.S. and Chilean governments relaunched their bilateral talks regarding a free trade agreement.

In conclusion, while in Argentina and Brazil political calculations about domestic stability became the driving forces behind economic liberalization and integration, in Chile the same political calculations about democratic consolidation led to a favorable, but more gradual and limited approach to economic integration because of structural economic differences. For the democratic Chilean government, its good economic performance was a priority as a crucial test of democratic legitimization and consequent consolidation, especially after an economically successful military regime, and integration could contribute to it if it was properly managed.

Therefore, in the end, the Argentine, Brazilian, and Chilean governments shared a common interest in the consolidation of the sub-regional Open Regionalism strategy, and its success became the main condition for the consolidation of their respective domestic political regimes.

---

[51] Chile's fourth democratic President since 1990, Ricardo Lagos, who assumed tenure on March 11, 2000, announced in July 2000 his government's disposition to continue the negotiations for full membership of MERCOSUR. See Southern Cone Report, 1 August (2000: 1).

## 3. The New Economic Interdependence in the Southern Cone During the 1990s.

The most significant feature of the 1990s Southern Cone convergence into economic liberalization was the sudden increase of economic and physical interdependence to levels that were--with different intensities--unprecedented in historical terms and were of strategic relevance in assuring mutual national welfare and economic growth. Thus, increased interdependence acted in favor of security cooperation in two directions: first, it changed threat perceptions. Second, it created the demand for new security regimes that would be able to shape the security of the changing economic and physical environment.

This section (3) details the levels of interdependence in terms of trade, intra-regional financial and direct investments[52], physical integration, and interdependence in strategic sectors, such as energy. The following section (4) describes the effects of increased interdependence on security cooperation.

### a. Trade.

Economic growth during the 90s in Latin America has been based on growth of the foreign sector, mainly of exports, which has "considerably surpassed GDP growth (...). Between 1992 and 1998, estimated average GDP growth was 3.6%, while export growth was over 9% and the average rate of growth in imports exceeded 12% (...). Latin America's exports grew at average rates of 9% in volume and 10% in value. These rates were exceeded only by China and the six highest growth economies in Asia"

---

[52] Although traditional commercial liberalism (Doyle 1997) and more recent democratic peace theories have focused on the importance of trade for peaceful inter-state coexistence (Doyle 1986), recent research has focused on financial integration, with similar conclusions, reinforcing the need of examining the importance of Southern Cone financial interdependence. See Gartzke *et al* 2001.

(ECLAC 1999: 21). As Figure 4 shows, the relevance of the export sector has increased during the 1990s as a consequence of the market reforms, and particularly relevant has been intra-regional trade increase in the Southern Cone, in both absolute and relative terms (Figures 5, 6, 7, and 8).

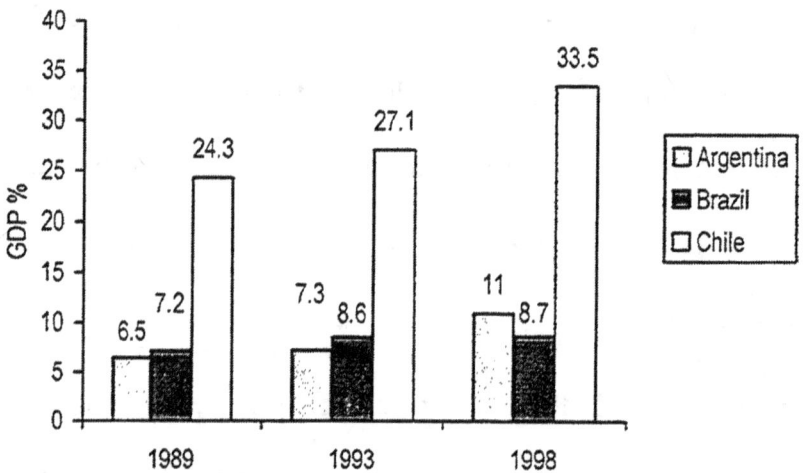

Figure 4. Selected Export Coefficients. Value of Exports as Percentage of GDP, in 1995 US$ Prices.

*(Source: author, based upon ECLAC 1999: 24)*

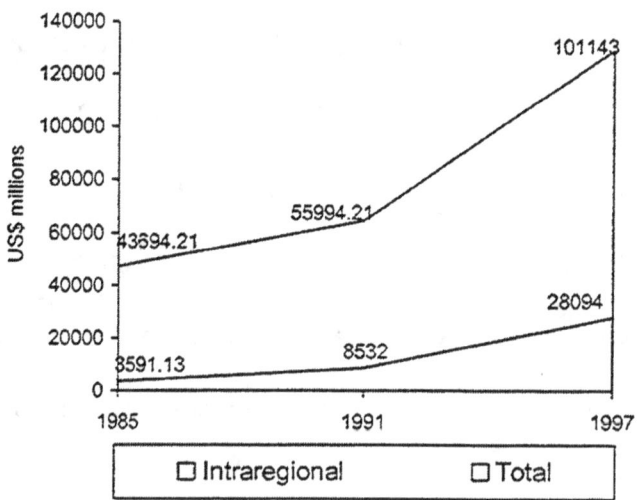

Figure 5. Mercosur, Bolivia, and Chile: Total and Intra-Regional Trade, 1985-1997
*(Source: author, based upon IMF Direction of Trade Statistics Yearbook)*

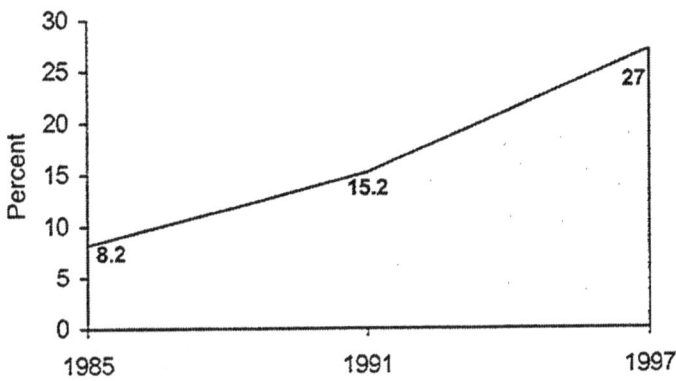

Figure 6. Mercosur, Bolivia, and Chile: Intra-Regional Trade as Percent of Total Trade, 1985-1997[53].

*(Source: author, based upon IMF Direction of Trade Statistics Yearbook)*

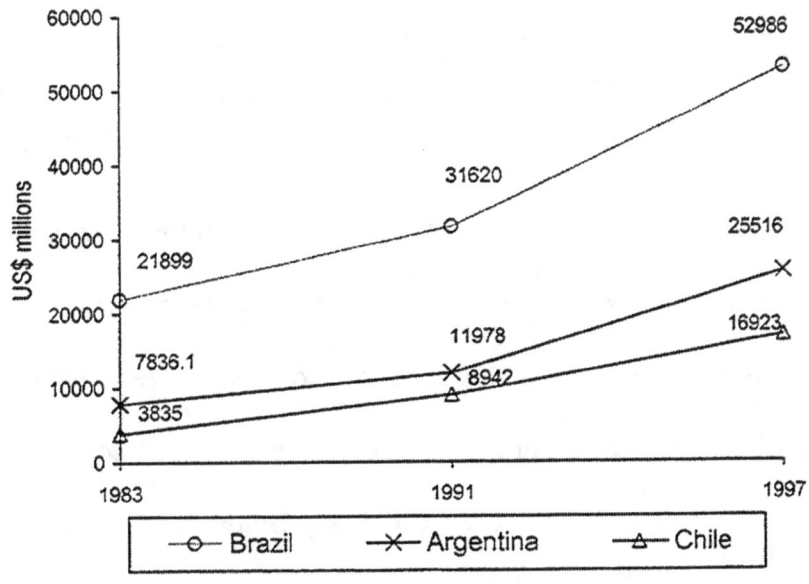

Figure 7. Argentina, Brazil, and Chile Total Exports, 1983-1997.

*(Source: author, based upon IMF Direction of Trade Statistics Yearbook)*

---

[53] We include Bolivia only because its association with Mercosur in 1996, almost simultaneously with Chile.

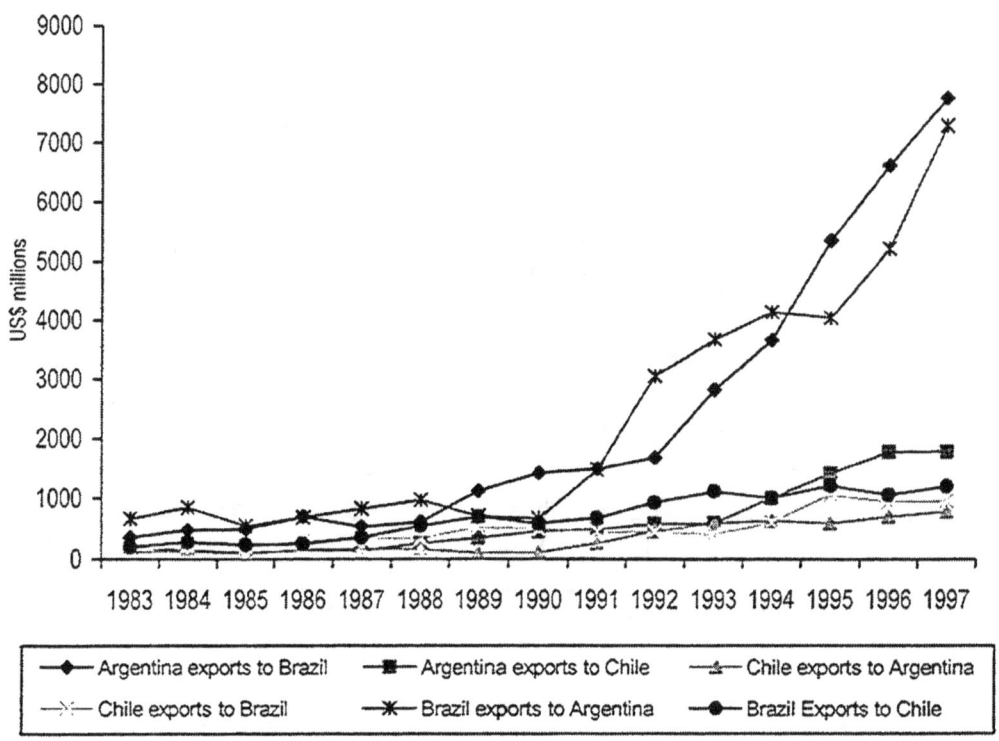

Figure 8. Trade Between Argentina, Brazil, and Chile, 1985-1997.
*(Source: author, based upon IMF Direction of Trade Statistics Yearbook)*

However, trade became not merely more important but crucial to the countries' welfare and, in this sense, strategic for the economic development of Southern Cone countries. Figure 9 illustrates the dimension of the shift and indicates that, for Argentina, Brazil accounts for a third of her exports and Chile is equal to the US as a market for her exports. Overall, Mercosur, Chile, and Bolivia (the so-called Mercosur + 2) account for 44 percent of her total trade. In the Brazilian case, Figure 10 indicates that while its exports were more diversified and Mercosur's importance was relatively minor, in 1998 Mercosur and Chile accounted for 22% of its exports, the same percent as the U.S. in the same year.

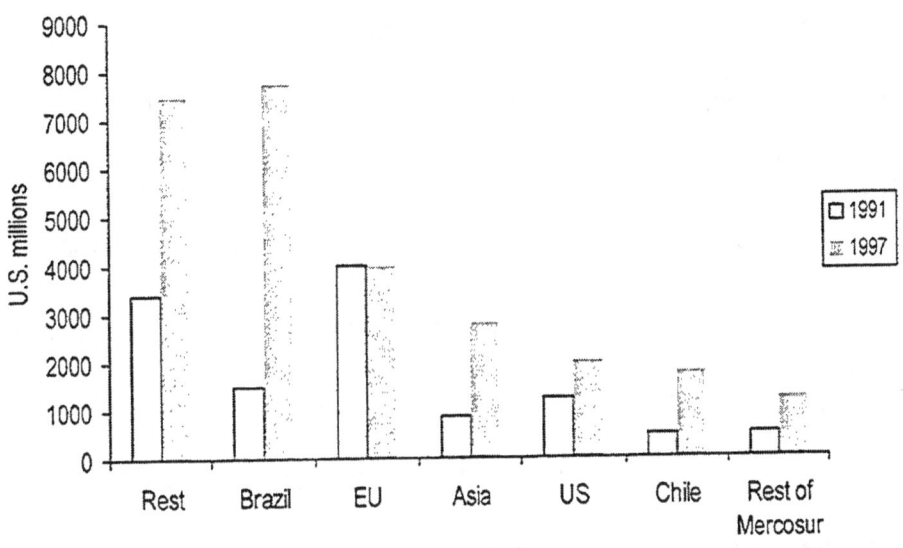

Figure 9. Argentina's Exports, 1991-1997.

*(Source: author, based upon IMF Direction of Trade Statistics Yearbook 1998)*

### b. Investment.

Within a context of market liberalization after a period of debt crisis and under a process of re-industrialization, foreign capital and technological investment remained vital for Southern Cone strategies of development. It is precisely in the area of foreign investment that some of the most innovative changes have happened in the Southern Cone during the 90s, because the sub-region began to experience significant levels of foreign investment from within the region for the first time in history. The key role has been played by the Chilean private sector. A few years after the Chilean state adopted its neoliberal economic model, it began to produce high rates of national savings as a result of the privatization of pensions. Consequently, Chilean entrepreneurs became highly interested in expansion and thus internationalization, of their investment portfolios. Chile is not the only intra-regional investor. Argentines and Brazilians have also invested in each other's country and in Chile, but Chilean investors have been by far the most significant. Figure 11 illustrates the total Chilean investment in October 2000. Chilean-executed investment in Argentina and Brazil corresponded to about 16 percent of Chile's GDP[54], and has been systematically developed.

---

[54] This estimation is based upon Chilean Central Bank information about Chilean foreign investment and U.S. Department of Commerce (2000) estimates of Chilean GDP.

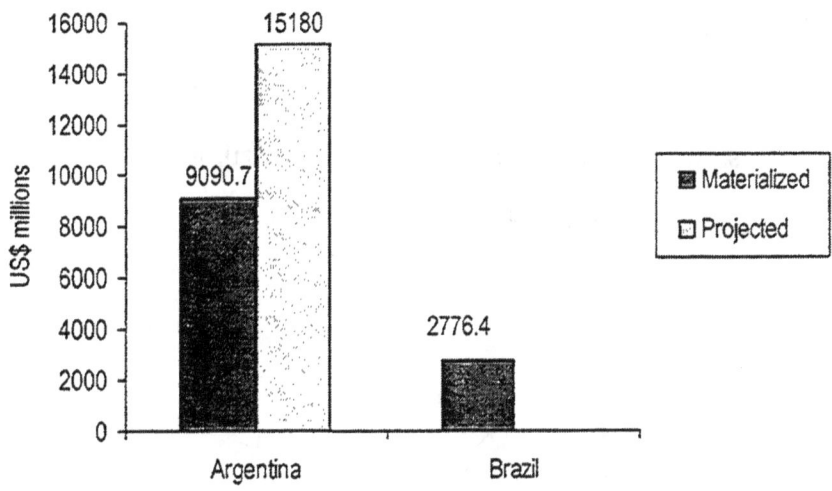

Figure 11. Chilean Investment in Argentina and Brazil.
*(Source: author, based upon Ministerio de Relaciones Exteriores de Chile 2001a[55])*

Of the three countries, Chile's private companies became by far the major

Southern Cone investors in the region, and this has increased interdependence to

unprecedented levels in the countries' history, especially because the larger investments

have been made in the countries that the traditional Chilean geopolitical thinking

considered rivals, particularly Argentina[56]. In addition, Chilean investment in the

Brazilian "Denationalization Plan" (DNP, privatizations), although secondary, was

significant. According to Guedes Da Costa, it was only 1.5% of its total, (US$ 1,006

millions), but more than that of France, Germany, Holland, British, Belgium, Sweden,

Japan or Canada, and inferior only to investment from Spain (14%), the U.S. (11.8%),

Portugal (7%) and Italy (1.8%), as shown in Figure 12. Finally, Chileans have invested in

---

[55] Projections for Brazil were not available. According to Cheyre (2000: 88), Chilean investments in Argentina were even bigger (US$ 11,109.3).

[56] Chile also became a major investor in the Bolivian and Peruvian processes of privatization and market deregulation during the 1990s.

diverse sectors[57] and usually as participants in wider alliances with local and transnational capital, creating multinational networks of sub-regional or regional dimensions that simultaneously operate not only in Brazil or Argentina, but also in other Latin American countries (Cheyre 2000: 88).

Photo Removed Due to Copyright Restrictions

Figure 12. Foreign Participation in Brazil's DNP.
*(From Guedes Da Costa 2000: 16)*

### c. Physical Integration, Energy, and Mining.

During the 1990s integration has also been deepened in physical infrastructure, energy, and mining, extending in these three sectors beyond the bilateral Argentine-Brazilian energy integration reached through the management of the Paraná River (the Itaipú Project), which made interdependent the industrial bases of southern Brazil and Buenos Aires, the two most significant economic zones in South America.

---

[57] According to Cheyre, Chilean private capital invested in Argentina was distributed among energy, industry, commerce, banking, insurance and pensions, and others, the sector represents the 46.1, 34.1, 10.7, 3.3, 1.0, and 1.3 percent, respectively of the total Chilean investment (2000: 88).

Physical integration was accelerated between Chile and Mercosur in the 1996 bilateral Treaty of Association, which contemplated the opening of twelve passes in the Chilean-Argentine border, aiming at the building of several inter-oceanic corridors[58] to connect trade between Mercosur and the Asia-Pacific Region. After several years of study within the Latin American Free Trade Association (LAFTA) and bilateral Argentine-Chilean and Brazilian-Chilean commissions, there are five corridors under construction, of which the main ones are:

1. Santos (Brazil)-Cáceres (Argentina)-Santa Cruz (Bolivia)-La Paz (Bolivia)-Arica seaport (Chile).

2. Santos (Brazil)-Asunción (Paraguay)-Antofagasta (Chile).

3. Valparaíso (Chile)-Buenos Aires (Argentina).

Chile and Argentina are also building three more corridors across their southern border: Corredor Sur (Pino Hachado border pass); Corredor de Los Lagos (Cardenal Samoré border pass); and Corredor Austral. According to estimations presented by Chilean authorities, the projected corridors will be more efficient in terms of time and costs than the current sea-lanes of communication (Quintana 1997).

The Chile-Mercosur Treaty of 1996 also prompted further integration in two other areas with not only economic but also strategic importance, energy and mining. Energy integration was prompted by the Chilean lack of reserves and rising demand spurred by its economic growth during the 1990s, and was made possible by the 1996 Treaty. As a result, in 2000, Argentine-Chilean enterprises built six gas pipelines, one

---

[58] Interoceanic corridors are "physical connections through several ways—highways, railways, and the Paraná hydroway--, which are complemented with an adequate institutional and administrative definition to allow the expedited operation of these routes" (Quintana 1997: 143).

poly-pipeline, and one oil pipeline to Chile. Secondly, a bilateral Chilean-Argentine agreement on electric interconnection was signed in 1997, and two lines were built, one under operation through Paso Huemules and the other under construction between Salta and Atacama (Ministerio de Relaciones Exteriores, 2000b). For Chile, Argentine is widely seen as the cheapest source of electric power in the long term, and this view is changing Chilean strategic planning, opening an alternative option to the construction of nuclear plants, which have been under study for a long time.

Mining integration was also prompted after 1996. On December 29, 1997, Argentina and Chile signed a bilateral Mining Integration and Complementation Treaty, which allowed joint exploitation of border deposits. The treaty was highly stimulated by the existence of projects worth of about US$ 6.500 million in the medium term (Ministerio de Relaciones Exteriores, 2000b). Other aspects of physical integration also deepened during the 1990s include increases in tourism and the gradual harmonization of several items of domestic legislation, especially those aimed at freeing the movement of persons among Mercosur, Bolivia, and Chile.

### 4. Effects of Increasing Economic Interdependence on Security Cooperation.

The changes in the economic relationship between Argentina, Brazil, and Chile have been made during a relatively brief period, especially since the Brazilian and Argentine economic liberalization processes began in the 1990s, but are qualitative. Economic integration and increasing interdependence introduced a strategic change in Southern Cone relationships through two causal mechanisms: First, by linking the countries' welfare to the deepening of a well-managed integration process, it modified the countries' *intentions* in relation to one another, thus leading to changes in threat

84

perception in their strategic thinking. Second, it increased the demand for regimes aiming to properly manage the new interdependent environment. Both dimensions will be analyzed in sequence.

### a. Economic interdependence and strategic changes.

From a conceptual point of view, the concept of strategy has experienced successive changes during the modern period, two aspects of which are pertinent to highlight. First, virtually all schools of thought have confirmed Clausewitz's basic and classic formulation of war (or the use of state external violence) as a means subordinated to the ends of politics (Clausewitz, 1993: 99, 146), but they have increasingly widened the scope of strategy from its purely military dimension, to include all the other dimensions that the state needs to consider for the eventual use of force in the pursuit of its interests (Murray and Grimsley 1994: 2), and during this process scholars have developed the concept of strategy toward formulas that better describe this widening scope. In 1991, for instance, Kennedy refined the concept of "Grand Strategy" as "the capacity of the nation's leaders to bring together all the elements, both military and non-military, for the preservation and enhancement of the nation's long-term (...) best interests" (1991: 5), which is very similar to the updated conceptualizations of security elaborated both internationally and in the Southern Cone[59].

Second, students of strategy also still support Clausewitz's original observation that the other's power "is the product of two inseparable factors, viz, *the total means at his disposal* and the *strength of his will*" [italics in the original]. As he

---

[59] In our opinion, the basic proposition made by Keohane and Nye (1977) that is, that under interdependent conditions there is no hierarchy among issues, and Buzan *et al*'s "new framework" for security analysis (1998), reflect a similar assessment. For close Latin American conceptualizations of security see Somavía and Insulza 1990.

formulated it, "the extent of the means at his disposal is a matter--though not exclusively--of figures, and should be measurable. But the strength of his will is much less easy to determine and can only be gauged approximately by the strength of the motive animating it" (Clausewitz 1993: 86). As some scholars have argued, one of the problems in strategic assessments is the trend to overemphasize the problem of the *means*[60], to the detriment of assessing "what others think, want, and can do" (Murray 1997: 63).

The changes in the models of development that Argentina, Brazil, and Chile have experienced since the 1990s are changes of "grand strategy", and they imply a change in the Clausewitz's subjective component of the strategic inter-state relationship. For the first time in their history Argentina, Brazil, and Chile no longer see one another as necessarily inherent rivals or enemies (as was the case under previous models of development). Instead, with different intensities, the governments of the ABC countries see their neighbors as increasingly crucial partners for improved national welfare, successful domestic democratic consolidation, and international insertion. In Clausewitz's terms, economic interdependence changed countries' *intentions* towards one another and, as will be seen below, created a framework within which military capabilities have been kept at levels consistent with defensive deterrent strategies. The change has been reinforced by the pre-existence of territorial satisfaction with the status quo (Kacowicz 1998: 114).

It is important to underline that the above-mentioned change in strategic perception has been explicit between the governments, especially in Argentina and Chile,

---

[60] The main international discussion has centered on the strategic consequences of the Revolution in Military Affairs, that is, the qualitative impacts of the current extraordinary technological change in the making of strategy (Krepinovich 1994, Owen 1996). For critical assessments see Murray 1997 and Freedman 1998.

the two countries most sensitive to strategic imbalances. According to the Argentine Defense White Paper, "Mercosur has become an element of stability, because the network of interests and relations that it generates deepens links of any kind and neutralizes tendencies toward fragmentation. In this new context, the old assessment of the neighbor as adversary and eventual threat to our security is replaced by another equation: his risks are now also our risks (…), and the rival of the past becomes today's ally, with or without legal instruments" (Ministerio de Defensa Nacional 1999a: 13). A similar assessment was made by the Commander in Chief of the Chilean Navy in 1999 during the main official speech he traditionally delivers. According to him, "countries face risks and threats, understanding by risk the existence, in another international actor, of the capacity or intention of causing damage to us, and by threat, the simultaneous presence of both: capacity and intention to cause damage to us". He added that, since the 1984 Treaty of Peace and Friendship with Argentina, "a new relationship with our neighbor is under construction, in which we are transitioning from threats to risks" (Arancibia 2000).

Furthermore, in the Argentine, Brazilian, and Chilean case it is even possible to empirically analyze the strategic change, examining both the *intentions*, measured in terms of defense policies (threat perception, conflict hypothesis, and strategic posture), and *capabilities*, measured in terms of military resources (military expenditure and the evolution of military capabilities).

(1) Defense Policies. In the case of Argentina, three periods can be distinguished. The first began with the changes introduced by the civilian political authorities during the Alfonsín government (1983-1990). Quoting former defense

87

ministers and military planners, Barletta asserts that "by 1988, military as well as civilian sectors in both countries [Argentina and Brazil] ceased viewing the others a security threat", leading to a revision of war plans (1999: 22). Although the change was pushed by civilians aiming to weaken domestic military rivals, the Argentine military institutions, represented by their chiefs of staff, accepted the shift, especially in the Army. In 1995 Lieutenant General Martín Balza, chief of the Army Staff, wrote that "between the countries of Mercosur there does not exist, and should not exist a conflict hypothesis", and proposed a cooperative security strategy (Balza 1995: 4). A second period was the promulgation in November 1996 of the *Directiva Para la Realización del Planeamiento Militar Conjunto* [Directive for Joint Military Planning], which maintains that "the regional integration processes diminish the possibilities of conflict". However, it asserts that integration does not exclude the existence of conflict, threats, and risks in the short, medium, and long term, which "will be determinant for the preparation, development, evolution, and eventual employment of the armed forces"[61].

A third, significant step was made in 1999 when the Menem government also published the first Defense White Paper (Ministerio de Defensa Nacional 1999a, 1999b) in the country's history, making explicit and public most of the Argentine threat perception and defense policy. Regarding threat perception, the main features of the book stated that Argentina did not have border disputes (1999a: 11) and that the traditional conflict hypothesis with Brazil was over (1999a: 10), noting that "all the border disputes with Chile" had been solved (1999: 20), while the dispute over the Malvinas Islands, Georgias del Sur and Sandwich del Sur "remains latent" (1999a: 21).

---

[61] As quoted by Saín (1999: 139).

The White Paper also stated that "conflictive situations" might emerge around the "Argentine Antarctic" (1999: 21) and expressed concern about the illegal exploitation of Argentine resources in the Argentine Economic Exclusive Zone (EEZ) (1999a: 20). According to the white paper new phenomena have emerged as "threats, risk factors and concrete sources of instability for the region", such as drug trafficking, organized crime, and illegal weapons traffic, which "associated with terrorism and guerrilla movements are present with diverse intensity in some areas of the region" (1999: 11). Argentina could be exposed to the "emerging threat of drug trafficking and other transnational phenomena" (1999a: 20). Mercosur had become an "element of stability because the network of interests and relations that it generates, deepens the links and neutralizes trends toward fragmentation" (1999a: 13). In terms of the strategic posture, the defense white paper stated that "the primary mission of the military instrument is to act in a deterrent form" (1999b: 1), but it did not mention whether the military strategy was offensive or defensive, an aspect that has received intense criticism within Argentina and no comment from Brazil or Chile. Law No. 24.948 of *Reestructuración Militar* [Military Reestructuring] later codified the exclusively "deterrent" character of the Argentine military posture. The omission on the defensive/offensive character of the Argentine military posture prompted a debate in the Argentine Congress, during which the Argentine government rejected the modification of Articles 2 and 19 (which speak of a "deterrent strategy") and their replacement by the alternative paragraph stating that the posture would be "a strategic attitude of non-provocative defense" (Scheetz 1998: 47-9)[62].

---

[62] For the concept of non-provocative or non-offensive defense see UNIDIR 1990.

The evolution of Brazil's defense policies evidences initial parallels with that of Argentina's, because of the bilateral understanding between Presidents Alfonsín and Sarney. That is, there was an initial period of strategic change in the nuclear field and the deepening of preexisting patterns of cooperation. However, Brazilian defense policy remained unstated and tacit, and there was not a unified civilian agency for defense policy under civilian control. President Fernando Henrique Cardoso adopted the main steps in this direction. In December 1996 the Presidency published the first defense white paper in the country's history (Presidência da República 1996[63]) as part of a wider process of reform in the defense sector that continued with the creation of the Ministry of Defense in June 10, 1999 (Ministério da Defesa 2001).

In terms of threat perception, the document asserted that in South America, democratization tended to reduce the probability of conflict occurrence, and that Brazil enjoyed a strategic "peace ring" made by Mercosur and the Amazonic Treaty of Cooperation. However, the country was not free of "risks". "Some" of these risks were "armed bands acting in neighboring countries in the Amazon borders, and organized international crime". At the same time, and given the uncertainties of the international system, defense policy and military instruments were of "capital importance for states survival as independent units". The defense policy must be sustainable and oriented toward self-protection, and its success "depends on the construction of a model of development that strengthens democracy, reduces social inequalities and regional disequilibria, and makes compatible the need for development with defense and diplomacy". Finally, it stated that the Brazilian strategic orientation was twofold: an

---

[63] Original six-page text is in Portuguese. All the translations in the thesis will be made by the author unless expressly mentioned.

90

active diplomacy pursuing peace, and "a deterrent strategic posture of defensive character", warning that "the defensive character does not imply that, in case of conflict, the armed forces must be strictly limited to defensive operations" (Presidência da República 1996).

In the case of Chile, the evolution of defense policy, threat perception, conflict hypothesis, and strategic posture during the 1990s exhibits much continuity but also significant changes. As explained before, this change began with the newly elected democratic government in 1990, although this also maintained very important elements of continuity with the previous authoritarian regime in foreign and defense policy[64]. However, since the second half of the 1990s, particularly since Chile in 1997 published its first defense paper, the *Libro de la Defensa Nacional*[65], there has emerged a new strategic assessment, especially regarding the integration process. The book stated that the Chilean defense policy was of "deterrent character and its fundamental orientation is defensive" (1997: 88) and indicated that Chile had neither aggressive purposes against any nation nor territorial claims within its neighboring environment. In relation to deterrence, it made explicit that "it is not limited to the defensive option in the strategic alternative between it [deterrence] and the offensive

---

[64] Van Klaveren observes that it was in the territorial and strategic policy areas "where are observable the major permanence and, up to a certain point, major consensus in the principles and basic definitions of Chilean foreign policy" (1997: 119).

[65] It is important to underline that despite their commonalities the three state documents are very different both in the methodology conducive to their publication, and in their conceptual density. While the Brazilian six-page paper was elaborated by the Presidency without major participation of the Brazilian defense community, the Argentine and Chilean books were the outcome of two-year workshops with intense participation of their respective governments, military, congresses, political parties, universities, and think thanks. The Chilean book has been considered the more conceptual (Mani 2000: 39).

91

option (…). The mere defensive option (…) may be insufficient" to deter an adversary (1997: 89).

In relation to Chilean threat perception and conflict hypotheses the book stated that the existence of conflict hypotheses among states should be recognized, but explained that "a conflict hypothesis is different from its probability of occurrence" and that "within a context of interaction and cooperation, that is, of peace, the probability of occurrence diminishes and this diminution stimulates, in turn, the will for identifying new areas of interaction and cooperation" (Libro de la Defensa Nacional de Chile 1997: 37). The book presented several assertions relevant to the regional and sub-regional changes. First, it positively assessed regional democratization, indicating that the historical record shows that democracy offers better conditions for peace and stability than other political regimes[66] (1997: 52). Second, the country's document assessed the impact of integration positively because integration empowers "the diplomatic and economic factors of power", improves the welfare of isolated regions[67], and creates "a better scenario to settle disputes". However, the book warned that increasing interdependence does not eliminate conflict by itself, that both can coexist and may evolve "positively, toward cooperation, or negatively, toward confrontation" (1997: 66). Thus, transparency was considered "the condition" for economic complementarity, political stability, and predictability in governmental behavior, but it was also pointed out that institutionalization and consolidation of those conditions are processes of uneven

---

[66] This thesis, partially resembling the democratic peace theory, can also be seen in Insulza (1998: 104).

[67] Given the vulnerabilities its particular geography presents (particularly lack of strategic deepness), Chileans have been sensible to geopolitical thinking, even during the post-1990 democratic period, when the Chilean Army proposed a policy of developing the "Interior frontiers", which was widely welcomed among civilian leaders. See Abad 1994, Libro de la Defensa Nacional de Chile (1997: 127-8).

rhythm and none of them is quick (1997: 65). Equally, changes in states' relative power were also considered important and conducive to more complex regional equilibriums (1997: 67).

However, a more precise (although unofficial) picture of Chilean threat perception emerges from public statements made by some relevant political officials and military chiefs. First, according to Frei's Defense Minister, neighboring countries continued to present risks. The Bolivian territorial claim persisted[68], and political leaders in Argentina and Peru had demonstrated the will to use force during the 70s (the Peruvian and Bolivian crisis with Chile), the 80s (the Beagle and Falklands/Malvinas), and the 1990s (Peruvian-Ecuatorian crisis in 1991 and 1995-99) (Pérez 1997: 5). Therefore, while political will might have evolved favorably to detente, intentions might change again and Chile must be prepared for this eventuality. Second, according to Frei's government's Foreign Affairs Minister (and Lagos' Minister of Interior), "the scenario in the next years will present problems related to collateral effects of growing interdependence between our countries (South America), or to the globalization of some processes, and less with traditional conflict hypotheses that fed tensions during the past. While some of these will endure, they will remain circumscribed because of the growing shared interests which already constitute the axis ordaining our relationships with Southern Cone neighbor countries"[69]. In this context, he mentioned several potential risks for Chilean vital interests:

---

[68] Bolivia is the only country non-satisfied with her territorial status quo in the Southern Cone, demanding the access to the Pacific Ocean, lost during the War of the Pacific. The Chilean government does not accept the existence of pending border issues arguing that Bolivia formally accepted the current borders in the 1905 Treaty of Peace. See Burr (1967: 257-9) and Ministerio de Relaciones Exteriores 2001.

[69] See Insulza (1998: 110). He precised that many of the security problems were "risks" and not

- Governance crises in neighboring countries and their extension to Chile through massive and unpredicted migrations carrying drug trafficking, money laundering, terrorism and corruption.

- Risk of an arms race in the region, especially within the context of domestic crises and strong economic asymmetries among neighbor states, which could lead to the temptation of diversionary wars[70].

- The involvement of South American countries, or some of them, in extra-continental alliances, which would contradict advances toward plain regional autonomy and political integration. The U.S. granting of Main Non-NATO Ally Status to Argentina in 1997 was seen as a "cause of concern" because it would mean the incorporation of foreign agents in the definition of security affairs in South America (1998: 112).

Finally, he mentioned three other risks related to the defense of democratic political regimes, the stockpiling of toxic waste within the region with cross-border effects, and the transport of radioactive material through southern sea lanes, which, together with over-exploitation of natural resources, was causing significant concern in costal countries. The mismanagement of a crisis could produce regional destabilization (1998: 112). In 1999, the Chief of the National Defense Staff, Vice

---

threats, because the former meant the existence of adversaries decided to use force to modify regional conditions.

[70] The Minister distinguished "normal, regular reposition of equipment", from arms race, which he defined as "massive acquisition and/or introduction of last generation weapons of high destructive power that would significantly alter the regional strategic balances" (Insulza 1998: 112).

Admiral Hernán Couyoumdjian[71], stated that "although the possibility of a conflict always exists, its occurrence probability is minor" (1999: 3).

In summary, Chilean defense policy is understood as transitioning from a first period of confrontation, to another featured by a "new agenda of cooperation" in areas in which Southern Cone countries face common challenges or in which problems are transnational and require cooperation, especially in protection of the environment, the Exclusive Economic Zones, and the Antarctic (Pérez Yoma 1997).

(2)     Military Expenditure. Military expenditures are often used as indictors of the relative importance countries assign to their defense in a given strategic context, which is reflected in resources allocation, although the theoretical debate around the variables that determine military spending remains inconclusive (Looney 2000: 437). After the 1970s and 1980s, when the sub-region experienced several crises and military expenditure was increased, from the 1990s Southern Cone levels have been reduced and remain relatively stable and low in international comparative terms. However, comparative measurements have proved problematic within the Southern Cone because of methodological differences. For reasons of impartiality and comparative standarization, the selected data are extracted from the Stockholm International Peace Research Institute SIPRI Yearbook series, and are shown in Figure 13 and Figure 14.

---

[71] The National Defense Staff is the main advisory joint military structure in the Chilean defense system. Its duty is to advise the Defense Minister and to conduct security and defense (strategic) planning. See Ministerio de Defensa Nacional (1997: 97-8).

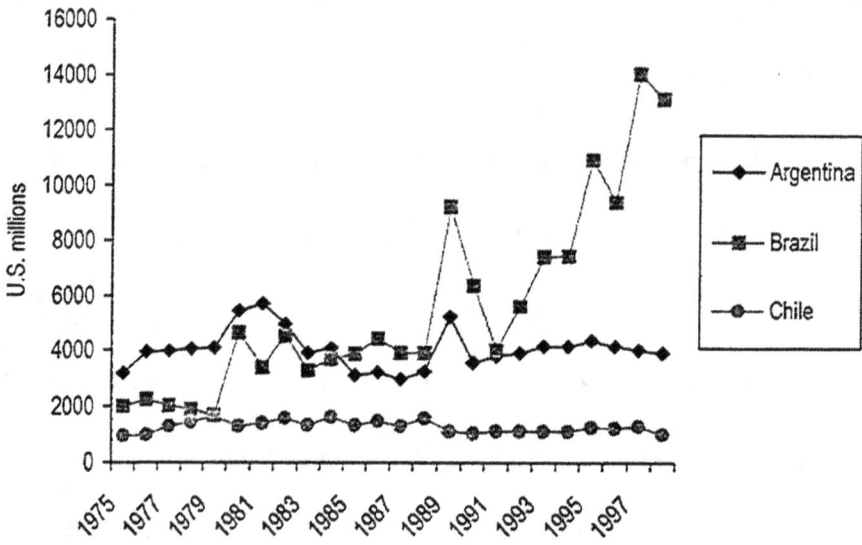

Figure 13. Absolute Military Expenditure, 1975-1998.

*(Source: author, based upon SIPRI Yearbook 1985, 1990, 1999[72])*

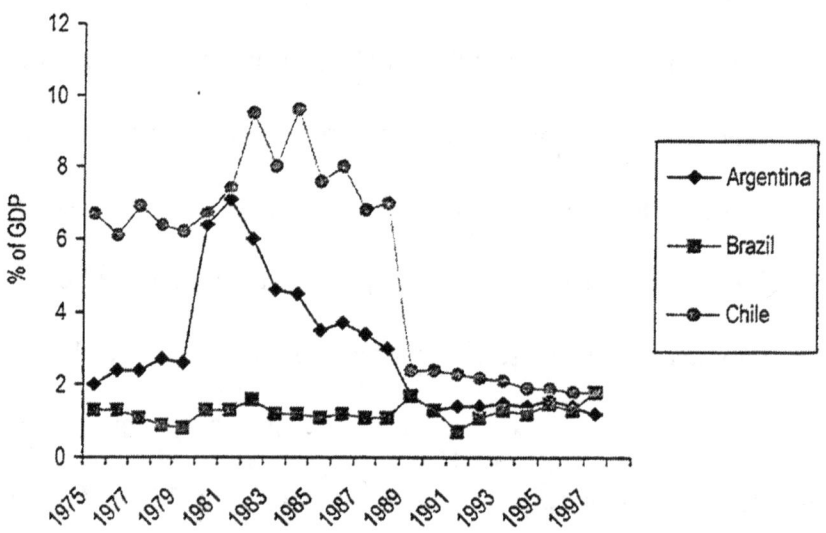

Figure 14. Relative Military Expenditure, 1975-1997.

*(Source: author, based upon SIPRI Yearbook 1985, 1990, 1999)*

---

[72] For the period 1975-1979 estimates are in US$ millions at 1980 prices and exchange rates. For the period 1980-1988 estimates are in US$ millions at 1988 prices and exchange rates. For the period 1989-1998 estimates are in US$ billions at constant 1995 prices and exchange rates for calendar year. The SIPRI does not provide a single methodology for the period.

As observed in Figure 13 and Figure 14, military expenditures were rising during the last period of the authoritarian regimes. In Figure 14 a Chilean and Argentine increase is observable which is contemporary to the Beagle Channel dispute. Absolute Chilean allocation reached its peak in 1979, while Argentine expenditure continued to rise during the Malvinas/Falklands dispute and began to decline after 1983, the year of democratization. Brazil's allocation followed the Argentine increase during the 1980s, but also declined after its democratization, in 1985, as did Chile's in 1990. However, during the late 1990s, and despite the budgetary shortages, Argentina still tripled the Chilean budget. The ratio was 3.4 in 1975, 3.3 in 1990, and 3.8 in 1999. Brazil exhibited a sudden increase in absolute terms, which is explained as the outcome of its economic recovery, and most of which went to personnel and operations.

The pattern during the 1990s is most stable in relative terms, as shown in Figure 14. Chile initially reduced its allocation, but since then has kept it relatively stable, as have both Argentina and Brazil. The three countries converge around more or less two percent of their GDP. Thus, defense expenditure remains at low levels and relatively stable, consonant with the improvement in the strategic southern Cone environment and security cooperation, although one may also observe much inertia (in Argentina and Chile) and a Brazilian increase that has not been perceived as threatening by Argentina. As will be seen below, this inertia partly related to low levels of civilian control over strategic planning, but it is also partly caused by civilian and military elites' tendency to agree that lower levels could threaten the deterrent character of their policies.

(3)		Military Capabilities. Military capabilities among Argentina, Brazil, and Chile have been traditionally asymmetric, particularly during the second half of the 20$^{th}$ century, and much of this period's history is the tale of Argentina's unsuccessful attempts to reach strategic parity with Brazil and of Chile's attempts to produce at least a credible deterrent regarding Argentina (as well as Peru and to a lesser extent, Bolivia)[73]. Most of the estimates converge, asserting that during the 1990s decade not much changed in relation to the above-described historical distribution of power capabilities. Acquisition programs have concentrated on replacement of systems completing their life cycles, which has been more difficult in the Argentine case because of economic difficulties. Also, most of the budgets are devoted to personnel (70-80 percent in the three cases), with secondary percentages going to operations and acquisitions. For instance, the IISS estimated in 2001 that "60% of Brazil's nearly 700 aircraft were not operational, mainly because of lack of spares" (IISS 2001: 221).

In the case of Argentina, despite it is being the most vocal supporter of sub-regional advances toward further integration, and even after the end of its compulsory military service, the country has basically maintained the same assets that it had before the 1990s, and many of its new systems have been provided by the U.S., such as 20 *A-4M* fighters and 8 *P3 Orions* purchased since 1999. However, its operational capacities have been reduced because of budgetary shortages (IISS 2001: 223).

Brazil has also maintained its strategic capacity during the decade, but in the late 1990s it began the processes to replace its fighters and also to replace its

---

[73] For extensive analyses of the strategic evolution of the Southern Cone see Tulchin *et al* 1998.

submarine forces through restarting its nuclear-powered submarine (SSN) program, which was conceived during the late 1980s as part of Brazil's defensive deterrent strategy[74]. According to the IISS, "Argentine naval activities provide a clue to why Brazil regards enhanced naval capabilities to be necessary. Argentina provided a frigate in the 1991 Gulf War, and in 2000 it provided a frigate to participate in the enforcement of the oil embargo against Iraq. This small contribution could reap important political benefits, particularly from the U.S. (...). Should the Brazilian Navy carry through its SSN program, it would become one of the only six navies able to deploy submarines worldwide, but it is difficult to find a military rationale for this capability. Brazil's naval ambitions are further underlined by its reported negotiations to buy the French aircraft carrier *Foch* to replace the ageing *Minais Gerais*" (IISS 2001: 221). Negotiations concluded successfully and the *Foch*, rechristened *Sao Paulo,* arrived at Rio de Janeiro on February 17, 2001 (Nomar 2001).

In the Chilean case, after lowering its military budget to stable levels, the country updated its ground, naval, and air forces relative to Argentine but also Peruvian levels. The Army replaced its main battle tank forces with 200 Leopard 1's delivered in 2000, the Air Force upgraded its fighters in Israel (F-5 and Mirage) and complemented them with early-warning systems and refueling capacities, while the navy began to replace its four submarines ordering four Scorpene units from France. The Navy is also planning to replace its ageing surface combatant forces (*Proyecto Tridente*) while maintaining the same number of ships (IISS 2001: 222). More controversial has been the long-announced acquisition of F-16 fighters (Cardamone 1997), a decision more

---

[74] For an analysis of the Brazilian nuclear submarine program see Barletta (2000:255).

understandable in the context of the Peruvian acquisitions during the 1980s and 1990s (Mirage 2000 and MIG 29) that gave Peru air superiority over Chile[75], but regarded with distrust by Argentina[76]. Figure 15, Figure 16, and Figure 17 partially illustrate the evolution of some indicators of military capabilities[77].

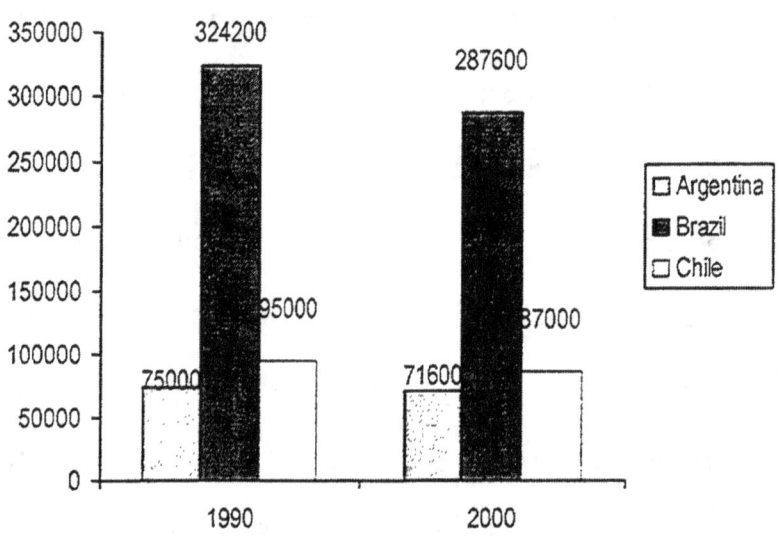

Figure 15. Total Active Manpower in Argentina, Brazil, and Chile, 1990-2000.

*(Source: author, based upon IISS Military Balance 1990-91, 200-2001)*

---

[75] Recent media information also shed light indicating that Peru equipped its Russian RSK MIG-29SE Fulcrum fighters with Vympel R-77 (AA-12 Adder), introducing the first Medium Range Air to Air Missiles (MRAAM) in Latin America. See Flight International 2001.

[76] Tibiletti and Donadio (1998: 110) noted that the early warning and refueling systems purchased by Chile during the 1990s "allow support for offensive actions in the midst of Argentine territory". However, Chile has had strategic capacity to reach Argentine strategic targets since the 1960s, when the United Kingdom transferred *Canberra* long-range bombers, whose life-cycle was well over in the 1980s. Chile's 1990s programs were designed to maintain similar strategic capacities without purchasing strategic bombers, and aiming to reduce its extreme geographic vulnerability (lack of strategic depth) in relation to Argentina.

[77] It is important to consider that Chilean forces are also designed to balance Peruvian capabilities, which are not considered in this study.

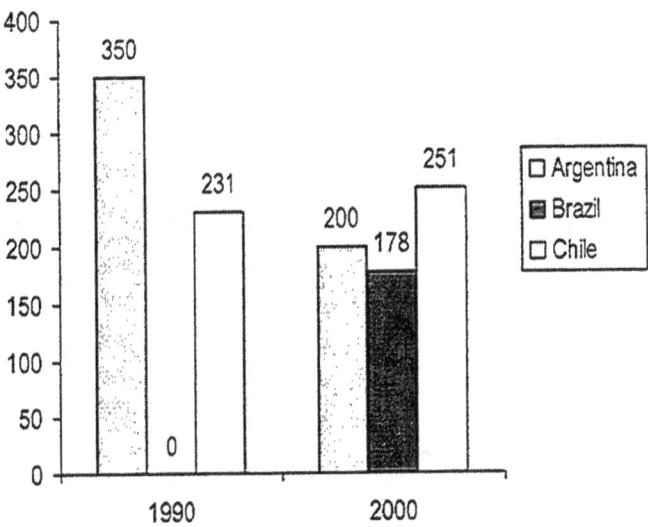

Figure 16. Argentine, Brazilian, and Chilean Main Battle Tanks, 1990-2000[78].

*(Source: author, based upon IISS Military Balance 1990-91, 200-2001)*

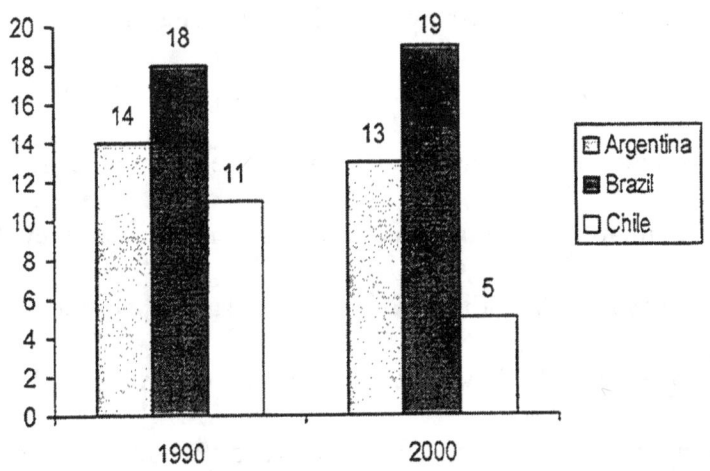

Figure 17. Argentine, Brazilian, and Chilean Principal Surface Combatants, 1990-2000.

*(Source: author, based upon IISS Military Balance 1990-91, 200-2001)*

Argentina has basically maintained its pre-1990 levels, while Brazil and Chile have begun modernization of their weapons systems. The asymmetry

---

[78] According to the IISS, in 1990 Brazil only had light tanks.

between Argentina and Brazil has been increased, while Chile has shortened its distance from Argentina. However, military capabilities remain basically defensive or for limited offense, and continue to be restricted to a great extent by the countries' GDP's differences, whose proportion in 1999 was 10 to 3.4 to 1.7 for Brazil, Argentina, and Chile[79], respectively, which is close to their proportion of absolute military expenditures in the same year: 10 to 2.96 to 0.78.

In summary, a change in the strategic relationship between Argentina, Brazil, and Chile is observable. Increased economic and societal interdependence has produced a change in their grand strategies, eliminating threat perceptions based on past territorial disputes and creating structural interests for strategies of cooperation. This change is measurable. Countries have made the shift explicit in their defense policies, and, although their defense expenditures and military capabilities exhibit some detrimental change in relation to the position Argentina had in the 1980s (after its most militarized period in history), they remain at low levels, and are consistent with defensive postures. In addition, shifts in military capabilities (such as the Brazilian and Chilean modernizations) have been deliberately de-dramatized because the gains from the changes in grand strategies and from increased economic cooperation have been far bigger than the partial losses in balance[80].

---

[79] The proportion is based on U.S. CIA estimates for 1999. See CIA 2001.

[80] In this respect we support Glaser's contingent realism, a structural realist approach to the problem of relative gains in cooperation first noted by Grieco (1988). According to Grieco, countries refrain from cooperation when the gains of the other are bigger. But Glaser points out that while this could be true if countries are concerned about gains in military or economic power (as traditional and structural realists argued), but not if the value at stake is security. If one's security is increased, the other's bigger security increase is not an obstacle for cooperation. See Glaser 1996.

### b. *Argentine, Brazilian, and Chilean Increased Interdependence and the Demand for Security Regimes.*

The literature tends to agree on the fact that increasing interdependence[81] does not necessarily mean more peaceful relationships between states (Keohane and Nye 1977: 7, McMillan 1997). In the ABC case, the second strategic dimension of increasing economic interdependence has originated in the need to coordinate the behavior of interdependent parties, in order to prevent decisions and processes being adopted or developed by one party that may affect the other(s), especially under asymmetrical conditions. The classic area in which intergovernmental regimes arise under increased economic interdependence is the economic field. However, the high levels of mutual dependence that Argentina, Brazil, and Chile have acquired during this period of increased interdependence also made it necessary to ensure that the most important components of each country's "grand strategy", especially those that may be perceived as linked to vital interests, are consonant with a non-aggressive relationship. Thus, as Pion-Berlin expressed, "to ensure its continued development, a state must not only learn to foster greater transparency in its economic relations with neighbors, but must ask its military to do so as well. As [...] civilian leaders come to believe that their countries' fates are inextricably intertwined, they will insist that their armed forces behave in ways that support peaceful coexistence" (Pion-Berlin 2000: 46) and are coherent with the implicit or explicit change in intentions.

---

[81] Keohane and Nye defined interdependence as a condition in which countries are highly sensitive and vulnerable to each other. "Sensitivity means liability to costly effects imposed from outside before polices are altered to try to change the situation. Vulnerability can be defined as an actor's liability to suffer costs imposed by external events even after policies have been altered".

Therefore, the new economic relationships have not only fostered security relations that are more consistent with increased cooperation, but have also demanded an increase in their transparency, and because of the non-hegemonic nature of the Argentine, Brazilian, and Chilean relationships, the more viable strategy has been the development of negotiated regimes focusing on conflict prevention mechanisms. In this sense, security regimes between these three countries have reduced uncertainty. It is no accident that during the 1990s they have developed an intense activity of regime building. This activity has aimed to reduce and prevent the re-emergence of past conflicts derived from territorial sources that could threaten the success of the new economic models and political regimes (Pérez 1997), and also to prevent the emergence of new conflicts caused by the increased economic and societal interdependence (Fuentes 1997, Avendaño 1997).

In a manner consistent with the above-explained dynamic conducive to increased demand for security regimes, Argentina, Brazil, and Chile evidence a notable increase in the amount and quality of bilateral and multilateral cooperative practices during the 1990s that have gone far beyond the levels previously reached.

(1)     Argentine-Brazilian Bilateral Security Cooperation. In the cases of Argentina and Brazil, since the end of the nuclear competition, both countries have maintained their collaboration in this area, especially regarding international negotiations on non-proliferation issues (Barletta 2000: 337), but have simultaneously extended it to non-nuclear security and military areas and institutionalized security cooperation at the military and, later, political levels. After establishing annual joint staff consultations in 1987, since the mid-1990s the armed forces are conducting joint military exercises with significant strategic symbolism that, at the same time, increased their

104

interoperability. In 1996 the two navies conducted two combined exercises in Argentine waters, while the armies conducted the "Operación Cruz del Sur", their first joint peacekeeping military exercise, which involved 1,500 troops and a significant amount of land and air means, weaponry, and logistics in northern Argentine territory (Caseros) under a single command. Also, in 1997 the navies of the countries conducted joint naval exercises, these being the first time that Argentine fighters landed on the Brazilian carrier *Minas Gerais*. In April 1997 both governments signed the Memorandum of Understanding, Consultations and Cooperation, establishing a permanent institutional bilateral mechanism of consultation in which the ministers of foreign affairs and defense and the military chiefs of both countries participate. During the same year, Brazil announced the reallocation of her military forces from the southern border with Argentina, to the borders of the Amazon region (Saín 1998: 136-7).

(2)     Argentine-Chilean Security Cooperation. After initial steps leading to some basic CBMs during the 1980s and early 1990's, previously discussed, since 1994 the Argentine-Chilean rapprochement has begun to exhibit a clear, second stage of higher levels of cooperation parallel to the Chilean shift in foreign policy toward Mercosur and the increasing levels of economic interdependence between 1990-1994, and following a similar pattern to that of the Argentine-Brazilian cooperation. In 1994 the annual meetings between joint military staffs were institutionalized as the permanent "Mechanism of Consultation and Coordination between the Armed Forces Staffs". In 1995 both governments instituted the Committee of Permanent Security (COMPERSEG in its Spanish acronym), bringing together political representatives of the Argentine and Chilean foreign and defense ministers and joint staffs, as a regular and

official forum for consultation on bilateral, regional, and multilateral security issues. Since them COMPERSEG has meet semiannually, each time in a different country. Since 1995 both countries have also begun to develop a set eight of new, more ambitious confidence-building measures (CBMs). They have also agreed to explore more advanced measures of confidence and transparency.

In July 1997 the Argentine and Chilean ministers of foreign and defense began to met annually, the first time in Zapallar, Chile, institutionalizing regular political consultations. As between Argentina and Brazil, the outcome was the structuring of a chain of consultations ranging from tactical-military cooperation and regular, bilateral inter-service meetings and consultations, through joint staff, high-level officials, and ministers, to presidents. The process begins in March with the military meetings and ends later in the year with presidential summits, which have been annual since 1994 (Ministerio de Defensa Nacional 1999), and it has produced an unprecedented frequency of diplomatic interactions between civilians and militaries of both countries, as well as a notable increase in the information flowing between both parties.

In December 1998 presidents Eduardo Frei and Carlos Menem reached agreement on the last and major pending border dispute in the "Agreement on Campo de Hielo Sur", ratified by both Congresses in June 1999, thus almost certainly closing the last border dispute[82]. Also in 1998, the Chilean and Argentine navies began joint Antarctic summer patrols, during which they alternate patrolling the waters between the continent and the Antarctic and providing logistic support for their respective

---

[82] The parties agreed on the definitive border for the southern part of the disputed zone. In relation to the northern part, the governments mandated their respective border commissions to establish a demarcation, after which a definitive proposal will be presented (Cheyre 2000: 32).

Antarctic bases. In 1999 the navies of Argentina and Chile signed the "Agreement on Joint Production of Naval Units", aimed at developing their naval industries and complementing each other's technological capacities. Under the agreement, during the same year the Chilean Navy Shipyards expanded the helicopter platform of the Argentine insignia warship, the *Hércules* destroyer, thus increasing its offensive operational capability[83]. This has been perhaps the clearest signal ever made by the Chilean state symbolizing its changing threat perceptions regarding Argentina. Also in 1999, the two governments decided to develop a common methodology to measure their respective defense expenditures and requested the United Nations Economic Commission for Latin America (ECLAC), as an impartial international organization, to develop it; the same year, Chile agreed to begin the gradual demining of their common border in the Southern region[84] (Ministerio de Relaciones Exteriores 2000b).

Finally, it is important to highlight that bilateral rapprochement between Argentina, Brazil, and Chile has also been reinforced by the countries' development or consolidation of several multilateral security regimes during the second half of the 1990s. For instance, Argentina and Chilean have played an important role promoting CBMs at the hemispheric level. In 1995 Chile hosted the First Regional Conference on CBM within the framework of the OAS and the Summit of the Americas Process, and both countries played significant roles in the second Conference, held in San Salvador, in 1998 (Cheyre 2000, OAS 2001b). Additionally, the three countries have also

---

[83] The expansion of the platform would allow the *Hercules* to carry heavy helicopters armed for anti-submarine warfare.

[84] Chile mined the frontier, especially during the 1970s, as part of its defensive military strategy. See Ministerio de Defensa Nacional 1997.

subscribed to 1997 Land Mine Convention, the 1997 Inter-American Convention Against the Illicit Manufacturing of and Trafficking in Firearms, Ammunition, Explosives, and Other Related Materials, and the 1999 Inter-American Convention on Transparency in Conventional Weapons Acquisitions.

**5. Conclusions.**

In sum, the analysis of the security and military relationships between Argentina, Brazil, and Chile during the 1990s (that is, the period during which the three countries were not only democracies but also converged on the adoption of market economies and economic integration) allows the following preliminary conclusions:

First, the new economic models consolidated the strategic change initiated during the 1980s, introducing an additional rationale for developing inter-state relations based on complementarity and, thus, on cooperation. Economic Integration ended--or at least substantially eroded--their traditional mutual threat perceptions and conflict hypotheses. This change is observable both in the now-explicit character of their defense policies and in the allocation of resources and the moderate evolution of their military capabilities.

However, it is important to highlight that the countries have not renounced the basic and traditional role of their armed forces. They continue to be the countries' primary foundations of national security, and deterrence continues to be the basic strategic posture, as shown in Table 1.

| Country | Strategy | Offense/defense character | Retains right to preventive strategic initiative |
|---------|----------|---------------------------|--------------------------------------------------|
| Argentina | Deterrence | Unstated | Unstated |
| Brazil | Deterrence | Defensive | Yes |
| Chile | Deterrence | Defensive | Yes |

Table 1. Argentine, Brazilian, and Chilean strategic postures according to their defense papers, 1996-1999.

The maintenance of credible deterrence must be understood within the new context created by increasing economic, societal, and environmental interdependence, which have generated new conflict hypotheses. To assert that Argentina, Brazil, and Chile have experienced a strategic change toward cooperation does not mean that they will never need military force to address conflicts that could emerge due to frictions over the management of the increased interdependence, especially with other states, in the region or outside the region, as will be seen in Chapter IV.

Second, during this period the consolidation of bilateral security regimes aimed at conflict prevention is observable. Historical border disputes have finally been solved between Argentina and Chile, intentions and capabilities have been made transparent through defense white papers and CBMs, and interoperability has been increased. In this way, the new regimes have reduced the cost of legitimate transactions, raised the cost of the illegitimate ones, and reduced the uncertainty of a period in which Argentina, Brazil, and Chile are more interdependent with each other than ever before.

To some extent, the type of security cooperation these countries have developed is close to the concept of cooperative security[85], especially in its preventive character. The re-deployment of military forces in Brazil is also consistent with this concept. However, at the same time, and despite Argentine proposals[86], neither Brazil nor Chile has assumed the doctrinal implications of this concept[87], and none of the three countries has demonstrated practical disposition to negotiate conventional arms controls[88]. During the period under study the more viable regimes seemed to be consensual agreements that adequately reflect the security concerns of the parties. In this sense, the adoption of more sophisticated security regimes seems to depend on how compatible they will be with the whole set of countries' national goals and policies, beyond the logic opened by economic cooperation.

---

[85] We refer to cooperative security as defined by Carter *et al*, in which "cooperative security thus displaces the centerpiece of security planning from preparing to counter threat to preventing such threats from arising–from deterring aggression to making preparation for it more difficult". It is "designed to ensure that organized aggression cannot start on any large scale" (1992: 191). To this end, "the only legitimate purpose of national military forces is the defense of national territory or the participation in multinational forces that enforce U.N. sanctions or maintain peace" (1992: 193), and they must be "structured for defense of national territory and their territory-taking capabilities for deep-strike at rear and homeland targets inside the territory of others by missile or long-range aircraft would be constrained" (1992: 194).

[86] In 1992 Carter *et al* argued that "the key to such international control would be the creation of an international surveillance system that maintained the current 'order of battle' of military aircraft on a world wide basis" (1992: 198). In 1998 Tibiletti and Donadio proposed the creation of a "joint system of electronic satellite intelligence able to detect and intercept any threats to the air space in the sub-region of the Southern Cone" (1998:111).

[87] Similar to the concept and doctrine of cooperative security coined by Carter *et al*, policies based on theories of non-offensive defense have also been proposed in Argentina. See Cáceres and Scheetz 1995.

[88] It is also important to note that the possibilities for Chile to develop cooperative security regimes are constrained by Santiago's strategic assessments regarding Peru and Bolivia. See Avendaño 1997, Pérez 1997, and Insulza 1998.

## C. CIVIL-MILITARY RELATIONS AND SECURITY COOPERATION: A COMPETING HYPOTHESIS.

In the analysis of the emergence of security cooperation in the Southern Cone several authors have argued with different degrees of emphasis that the possibility of significant advances in the sub-regional security cooperation has been shaped not only by the political will of the countries' democratic leaders, but also by the institutional distribution of power between the newly elected civilian governments and the military. According to this thesis, where the military prerogatives[89] were strong, the traditional military geopolitical perspective would prevail and security cooperation would be resisted. The critical factor defining the domestic balance of power is said to be the institutional arrangements resulting from each democratic transition. Argentina was the country that presented lower levels of military prerogatives, Brazil began its democracy at an intermediate level, while Chile presented higher levels. Consequently, the more advanced levels of security cooperation and economic integration reached by Argentina and Brazil in comparison to Chile, as well as the Chilean distance regarding Mercosur, were seen as the confirmation of the institutionalist thesis (Linz and Stepan 1996, Hunter 1996, Hirst 1998: 110, Escudé and Fontana: 65-70, Pion-Berlin 2000, Agüero 2000).

Historical institutionalist approaches have been partially correct but flawed. They can explain the initial increase in the Argentine-Brazilian case, that is, the first phase of the strategic change in the Southern Cone, especially in the Argentine case, because

---

[89] According to Stepan's seminal definition, "military institutional prerogatives refers to those areas where, whether challenged or not, the military as an institution assumes they have an acquired right or privilege, formal or informal, to exercise effective control over its internal governance, to play a role within extramilitary areas within the state apparatus, or even to structure relationships between the state and political or civil society" (1988: 93).

111

diminished military prerogatives increased Alfonsín's maneuvering room. However, they are not able to explain why, if the Brazilian military had higher prerogatives, President Sarney could favorably respond to the Argentine proposals, or how the increase in security cooperation between Argentina and Chile could finally be reached before and during the 1990s[90], especially during the second period featuring economic liberalization. In other words, the historical institutionalist focus on institutional power distribution leads to overlooking changes in preferences of the military and important departures from traditional geopolitical perspectives.

Historical institutionalist arguments do not correctly describe the Chilean dynamic regarding integration. Although military prerogatives are important in Chile, they have not been used to shape the integration process. Instead, the President has an overwhelming room of scope for maneuver regarding economic, foreign, security, and defense policy-making[91]. Some services, such as the Army, have been more institutionally laggard in executing the policies decided by civilian elected officials[92], but they have not, as institutions, publicly contested the new policy. Second, the strategic thinking of the Chilean armed forces has experienced a transition toward a more favorable approach regarding integration and security cooperation. This was reflected during the military's participation in the 1996-1997 workshop leading to the Book of the

---

[90] For a theoretical debate about different types of institutionalism see Steinmo and Thelen 1992. For critical assessment of historical institutionalist theories in relation to Latin America see Hunter 1997, Weidner 2000, and Atria 2000.

[91] For contending assessments of the institutional prerogatives between the President and the Chilean military, see Loveman 1991, 1994, García and Montes 1994, Ensalaco 1995, Ministerio de Defensa Nacional 1997, Gazmuri 1997, and Atria 2000.

[92] The Chilean Navy and the Air Force were the first services to fully execute the set of eight CBMs agreed by the Argentine and Chilean governments in 1995, including the realization of the first combined military exercises since 1997. However, the Army delayed the execution until 1999.

National Defense, which adopted a cautious but favorable approach regarding integration (Ministerio de Defensa Nacional de Chile 1997: 66-7)[93]. Reflecting the two-year debate among 120 high civilian officials, high officers invested with formal representation of their military institutions, congressmen, representatives of political parties, think thanks, and universities, the Book finally became "one of the country's most consensually crafted state documents" (Gaspar 1999: 186) and reflected that despite their recent domestic conflicts and the institutional weaknesses of their democratic regime, Chileans continue to exhibit a high degree of continuity and homogeneity in their foreign and security policies (Van Klaveren 1997: 119).

Therefore, intense security cooperation has been developed among Argentina, Brazil, and Chile despite the fact that the countries exhibit different levels of civilian control over the military. The military has not restricted or vetoed the foreign policies of economic integration and security cooperation developed by democratic civilian leaders in any of the three countries. On the contrary, in these three cases the processes of integration have sparked unprecedented civil-military dialogues on foreign and security policies that have reduced previous civil-military distrust and misperceptions, and in some cases, such as Chile, have even opened the way for further advances in the more sensitive areas of human rights and institutional reforms (Robledo 2001).

The previous assertion does not mean that non-democratic institutional constraints cannot play a role in the future and that civilian control does not need to be improved in these countries. In the ABC there is still a wide margin of military autonomy, especially

---

[93] The most recent military literature reflects an evolution in the military thinking toward a more balanced, favorable assessment of the integration process. See Arancibia 2000 (Commander in Chief, Chilean navy); and Molina 2000 (Chief of Operations, Chilean Army).

in critical areas of defense policy-making such as budgeting, doctrines, strategic planning, and force structure (Hunter 1997, McSherry 1997, Cruz and Diamint 1998, Rojas 1998a, Zaverucha 1998, Saín 1999, Scheetz 1998, Fuentes 2000, Atria 2000, Robledo 2001). In the Argentine case, for instance, civilian control over the military has been reached based on "sanctions and appeasement" (Trinkunas 2000), and security policies have been planned and executed through "circumvention" of the Ministry of Defense and the Armed Forces (Pion-Berlin 1999). Thus, if the integration process continues, political concertation and security cooperation are enhanced, and civilians attempt major changes in force structure, doctrines, and resource allocations, the military might eventually choose to exercise their prerogatives and to resist such changes. This may occur, for instance, if civilian governments agree to negotiate some type of sub-regional conventional arms control regimes. At this point, historical institutionalist approaches will be important to understand part of the dynamic in the ABC security cooperation.

# IV. MERCOSUR AS AN INTERNATIONAL ACTOR. INCENTIVES AND OBSTACLES FOR ADVANCES FROM CONFLICT PREVENTION TO COLLECTIVE ACTION IN SECURITY AFFAIRS.

As seen in the previous chapters, security cooperation among Argentina, Brazil, and Chile originated in and has been consolidated by the search of the new democratic governments for strengthened domestic stability, both directly, through security cooperation, and indirectly, through economic liberalization and economic integration. It has permitted the evolution of security cooperation from a first phase of conflict management, to a second focused on conflict prevention.

This chapter will address the question of how far this cooperation can go from its current stage. Despite Mercosur's clear intergovernmental character and complete absence of supranational decision-making bodies, its formation "naturally opened the question of whether there is any spillover effect into the realm of defense and security" (Pion-Berlin 2000: 43), leading to some type of common foreign and security policy.

We argue that an increase in the quality (and not only in the amount) of security cooperation could be prompted by three different dynamics. The first one is the adoption of some type of security regimes that are oriented to address transnational problems affecting the interests of the parties in the sub-region, especially those related to the protection of the environment, and that require inter-governmental coordination to be addressed. Important steps have been advanced bilaterally in this direction, especially between Argentina and Chile, and there is some evidence indicating that they can be addressed multilaterally. To be successful, however, this first scenario will depend more on shared threat perceptions by the three countries, which is still unclear. The second potential source of security cooperation emanates from the partial and gradual convergence of Argentina, Brazil, and Chile, on strategies aimed to maintain international peace and stability. Finally, the third dynamic that could foster security cooperation would be the eventual consolidation of Mercosur as an international actor projecting a common foreign and security policy. These are different scenarios, and all of them have germinal manifestations, but they share one common feature: all of them represent some type of collective action between Argentina, Brazil, and Chile to address security problems originating in sources other than inter-state Argentine-Brazilian-Chilean conflict. In this sense, they would represent a new phase of security cooperation. However, the third scenario rests on two assumptions: first, that countries develop convergent foreign policies and second, that Mercosur is consolidated as an international economic and political actor. As will be examined in this Chapter, both assumptions are problematic, which makes further advances in security cooperation--or security spillover--, still very uncertain and not mechanical.

Therefore, this Chapter will address the eventual emergence of a more advanced security cooperation, assessing the countries' incentives and constraints in the foreign policy area and the economic evolution of the economic integration process.

## A. THE 1990'S INTERNATIONAL SYSTEM AND THE FOREIGN POLICIES OF ARGENTINA, BRAZIL, AND CHILE.

The processes of economic integration and political association developed during the 1990s in the Southern Cone, especially during the second half of the decade, were developed in a very different international context than the previous process of security cooperation initiated by Argentina during the 1980s.

116

Perhaps the most important fact regarding Southern Cone cooperation is that the post-Cold War international system created strong incentives for increasing international activism in international security affairs. Not only is the international system more interdependent because of globalization, but because of the Argentine, Brazilian, and Chilean shift toward export-led models and the increasing openness of their economies, they are more vulnerable to the impact of financial fluidity than before, and they--especially Argentina and Chile--are also far more interdependent with several regions in the world. Therefore, they are much more interested in the maintenance of stability in the areas with which they have increased relations or in which they see their interests at stake.

The vulnerabilities emerging from increasing international interdependence have also been complicated by the fact that, while the international system has changed during the 1990s, the international regimes or institutions inherited from the Cold War designed to deal with international economy or security, such as the Bretton Wood institutions or the United Nations, respectively, have evidenced important shortcomings in their efficacy (and consequent legitimacy) when trying to manage financial crises, facilitate international trade, or address major post-Cold War conflicts[94]. Many of the difficulties in the development of new or reformed regimes come from changes in the international distribution of power, particularly from the continuing erosion of the U.S. hegemony (Keohane 1984) even after the end of the Cold War (Layne 1997: 244), from the proliferation of international actors with global capacities other than the states (and the

---

[94] The most common criticism of the U.N. rests on its inability to cope with the proliferation of intra-state conflicts featuring the post-Cold war international system and the scarce traditional inter-state conflicts during this period. According to SIPRI (1999: 18), of the 27 major armed conflicts in 1998, only two (India/Pakistan and Eritrea/Ethiopia) were interstate.

consequent relative fragmentation of the centers of international power), and from the increasing transnationalization of the international agenda; however, the combined effect of these changes has produced a global scenario in which the most successful strategies for regime building (when regimes are viable) are those which are based upon cooperative practices and whose viability depends to a great extent on international political leadership rather on the mere use of force (Keohane and Nye 1977).

In the security realm the U.N. system has experienced significant difficulties in trying to address the most important threats to international peace and stability during the post-Cold War period. The most visible outcome of this crisis has been the emergence of political responses outside the U.N. regime, such as U.S.-led unilateral humanitarian intervention in Kosovo[95], which have been criticized by Russia and China but tacitly accepted as legitimate by several other states given the U.N. paralysis regarding this and other crises (Glennon 1999). However, at the same time, because the weakening effects of this crisis on the whole U.N. system, it has also sparked a renovated activism in several countries trying to increase their participation in the U.N. security system, but also trying to reform the regime to address security problems through a more internationally regulated use of force (Rotfeld 1999).

In the economic realm, the global trend allowing cooperativism in regime building has been accompanied by the consolidation of the market economy as a global

---

[95] During 1999 the United Nations experienced its most serious crisis of credibility in relation to the purposes for which it was created and the mandate of the 1945 Charter of San Francisco. While ethnic cleansing was ongoing in Kosovo, the organization became paralyzed between non-intervention principles and humanitarian action regarding the genocide. Given the interests at stake for Europe and the United States, the U.N. paralysis led to an illegal, unilateral intervention of the North Atlantic Treaty Organization (NATO), which was heavily criticized by Russia and China, but seen as at least partially legitimate by an important number of states. See Glennon 1999.

paradigm, thus strengthening the process of international trade deregulation began after World War II under U.S. hegemony (World Bank 2000: 53). However, this trend in world trade has been executed not only through multilateral liberalization, but also through regional regimes, which imply more protectionist standards and are conceived as a strategy for two different scenarios. In the first one, regionalism may strengthen countries' negotiating position regarding further deregulation[96]; thus, it may be compatible with increasing international liberalization. In the second scenario, which assumes that multilateral negotiations for further liberalization fail and hostile inter-regional disputes arise[97], regionalism is, at least, a strategy that may keep a wider market open to the countries' economic activity. Therefore, despite the facts that the degree of liberalization or protectionism in the world economy is still not clear and that it is still not clear whether regionalism will help or further complicate international liberalization (Wyatt-Walter 1995: 116, Lindert and Pungel 1996: 221, Gillis *et al* 1996: 501-35), regionalism is increasingly adopted by the most dynamic economic regions in the world and, in this sense, is a consolidated international trend[98].

Thus, the above-described context has stimulated Argentine, Brazilian, and Chilean cooperation through two different but complementary dynamics. On the one hand, Argentina, Brazil, and Chile exhibit a gradual increase in their involvement in the United Nations (U.N.) security institutions, which has led to practices that influence

---

[96] This is the Open regionalist approach, which sees the creation of regional blocks as intermediate stages toward further international liberalization. See ECLAC 1994, Mols 1996, Bergsten 1997.

[97] This was the scenario that dominated the analysis of the international economic system after the 1970s (Thurow 1992), and before the success of APEC in 1993, which diminished fears of U.S.-Japanese disputes and prompted the final agreement in the Uruguay Round of the General Agreements of Tariffs and Trade (GATT). See Wyatt-Walter (1995: 118) and Bergsten (1997: 555).

[98] Fifty-two percent of world trade was intra-regional in 1990 (GATT 1992: 8), and between 1990 and 1998 regional trading arrangements came into force, more than ever before (World Bank 2000: 54).

security cooperation in the sub-region. Countries have participated in U.N. security institutions for different reasons. From the Brazilian perspective, as President Fernando Henrique Cardoso expressed it, "there is no alternative to multilateralism. Without it, we would run the permanent risk of a deterioration in the world order, leading to unilateralism and the law of the jungle" (Cardoso 1999:8). Argentina (as will be explained below) has experienced a shift in her historical foreign policy of autonomy toward bandwagoning with the U.S., especially in its political initiatives within the U.N. security system.

The outcome has been that during the 1990s the three countries have substantially increased their participation in U.N.-sponsored peace operations[99], Argentina in 1991 (Lagorio 1998) and Chile in 1999 (Fernández 2001) having advanced toward peace-enforcement operations[100], while Brazil has avoided participating in peace enforcement operations but has simultaneously increased its presence in peacekeeping operations. Gradually, and despite different foreign policies, the three countries have converged on a strengthened commitment to the maintenance of international peace and are increasingly interested to project some minimal level of force to support their limited but almost global interests, and even to increase their interoperability to eventually participate as joint forces in peace operations. Not surprisingly, when the Peruvian-Ecuadorian conflict over the Cenepa river re-erupted in 1995, they were not only the Guarantors of the Rio

---

[99] The two main types of U.N. sponsored peace operations are those involving the deployment of a U.N. force with the consent of the parties in a conflict--the classic peace keeping--, and those involving the use of force without the consent of one or more parties. The former are regulated by Chapter VI and the latter by Chapter VII of the United Nations Charter. See LeRoy (1995:466-97).

[100] In the Argentine case the country began its shift by participating in the 1991 Gulf War with naval support in the area. Chile has a long tradition of peacekeeping operations since the creation of the U.N., but since 1999 a Chilean Army company has participated in the U.N. force in East Timor, which was established by the Security Council under Chapter VII of the U.N. Charter. See Fernández 2001.

Protocol of 1942, but they were also in technical positions to play a much more active role than in previous crises, sending peacekeeping forces of proportional dimension to their political commitments to the solution of the bilateral dispute[101]. Therefore, a new space for security cooperation has been opened in the Southern Cone, and as was seen in Chapter III, the three countries have been increasing their interoperability since the late 1990s, aiming at eventual joint participation in peace operations.

Also, Mercosur was devised as an alternative economic strategy to the ISI model for the ABC countries' insertion in the international economy, and since 1995 member countries have relied on Mercosur as *de facto* international actor regarding economic negotiations with other regions. Importantly, the international agenda of Mercosur has been expanded and the countries have began to increasingly value the potential of Mercosur as a regime of intergovernmental political concertation regarding not only economic but also political negotiations with international powers and other regional groups. This trend has been visible since 1991, but in 1996 the group formally instituted its "Mechanism of Political Consultation and Concertation", and the examination of its agenda reveals a clear expansion from the merely economic aspects of the sub-regional economic integration to a wider range, including not only region-to-region trade but also political negotiations. Until 2000 Mercosur's external agenda was organized in the manner shown by Table 2 (for a detailed examination see Appendix 1):

---

[101] The peacekeeping force was integrated by the U.S., Argentina, Brazil, and Chile, the countries acting as guarantors of the 1942 Río Protocol between Ecuador and Peru. For the history and the strategic implication of the dispute during the 1990s see Marcella 1995. For the resolution of the conflict, see U.S. State Department 2001.

| Actor | Issue |
|---|---|
| WTO | Mercosur is coordinating its position as a block. |
| The G-7 | Mercosur had its first meeting with the club of industrialized economies in 1996 at Florence, Italy, during which the Brazilian (and also the Chilean) president advocated an improved international regulatory regime regarding financial globalization. |
| Europe | Mercosur is negotiating an association agreement with the EU, and an eventual economic agreement with the European Free Trade Area (EFTA). Formal talks have begun with the Russian Federation. |
| Americas | Mercosur has negotiated as a group since 1997 regarding the Free Trade Area of the Americas (FTAA). Also negotiates with the Andean Community, the Central American Common Market, and Mexico. |
| Asia-Pacific | Talks with have been held the Association of Southeast Asian Nations (ASEAN). Mercosur is developing talks with Australia and New Zealand, Japan, and India. |
| Africa | Mercosur is exploring an agreement with the Southern African Development Community (SADC)[102]. |

Table 2. Evolution of Mercosur's Political Concertation.

Also worth noting is the correlation between the gradual development of Mercosur's political cooperation in the above-mentioned areas of international politics, and the emergence of multilateral forms of security cooperation. Since the late 1990s, Mercosur's intergovernmental political concertation has come to include a gradual incorporation of security issues within the agenda, especially after the association of Chile and Bolivia. The milestones in the incorporation of security cooperation into the agenda of Mercosur and its Mechanism of Political Consultation and Concertation (which includes Chile and Bolivia) have been as Table 3 indicates:

---

[102] South African Presidents Nelson Mandela and Thabo Mbeki attended Mercosur's presidential summits in Ushuaia, 1998 and Florianapolis, 2000, respectively. See Mercosur 2001. For preliminary assessment of the Mercosur-ASEAN and SADC relationships see Lechini 1998 and Costa (1999: 119).

| Year | AREA |
|------|------|
| 1996 | Presidents of Mercosur, Chile, and Bolivia state their support for Argentine rights and claims over the "Malvinas Islands". |
| 1997 | Presidents instruct Ministers of Justice to accelerate the harmonization of domestic law between Mercosur, Chile, and Bolivia "in all the areas of the fight against organized crime". |
| 1998 | Mercosur, Bolivia, and Chile adopt the "Political Declaration of Mercosur, Bolivia and Chile as Zone of Peace". The presidents:<br>-Declare peace as "essential" to develop and continue regional integration.<br>-Commit to strengthen the mechanisms of consultation and cooperation on security and defense issues currently existing between its members and to **promote their progressive articulation** *[emphasis added]*.<br>-Commit to make efforts at international forums to advance toward international agreements aiming to achieve nuclear disarmament and non-proliferation in all of its aspects. |
| 1999 | Uruguay, on behalf of Mercosur, intervenes at the 54th U.N. General Assembly (October), expressing concern about the transit of radioactive material through sea-lanes of communication close to territorial waters and/or the Economic Exclusive Zone. |
| 2000 | Presidents of Mercosur, Bolivia, and Chile reaffirm their commitment to disarmament and non-proliferation of weapons of mass destruction, and agree to:<br>-Support the advances of the Non-Proliferation Treaty (NPT) Revision Conference.<br>-Support the advances of the ad hoc group of the Biological and Toxic Weapons Convention (BTWC).<br>-Welcome the fact that all South American countries ratified the Chemical Weapons Convention (CWC).<br>-Underline the importance of deepening efforts and initiatives toward transparency regarding conventional weapons, and call for universal participation on the U.N. Conventional Weapons Registrar.<br>-Express their intention to promote common efforts against drug trafficking and transnational crime.<br><br>Ministers of Interior of Mercosur, Bolivia, and Chile agree on plans for reciprocal cooperation and coordination regarding:<br>-Child trafficking.<br>-Economic-financial crimes.<br>-Illicit traffic in nuclear and/or radioactive material. |

Table 3. Evolution of Southern Cone Mutilateral Security Cooperation.

As can be seen, the group has articulated a basic agenda in which some issues are aimed to consolidate each country domestically (especially against drug trafficking and organized crime), but at the same time the others tend to consolidate the group's interests regarding the international system through intergovernmental coordination regarding non-proliferation, regional security, and protection of the environment and seas. In our opinion, 1998's "Declaration of Mercosur, Bolivia and Chile as Zone of Peace" introduced for the first time a basic disposition to increase sub-regional security cooperation building upon existing bilateral regimes, and the language is careful in this sense by resolving to "strengthen the mechanisms of consultation and cooperation on security and defense issues currently existing between its members and to promote their progressive articulation".

In conclusion, the evolution of the international system has been an important incentive inducing the evolution of Mercosur from an exclusively economic integration process, toward a sub-regional regime that the countries consider could facilitate the achievement of significant foreign policy goals, which include increasing levels of security cooperation.

However, as previously explained, the potential for political and security cooperation will depend to a great extent on two factors. The first is the extent to which Argentina, Brazil, and Chile can harmonize their foreign policies. The second is the consolidation of the customs union, which provided the basic rationale for the behavior of Mercosur as an international actor and which differentiates the group as a distinctive decision-making core even among the regional intergovernmental regimes of political concertation, especially the Rio Group. The former will be examined in section B, and the latter in section C.

## B. ARGENTINE, BRAZILIAN AND CHILEAN FOREIGN POLICY DIVERGENCES AROUND THE U.S.

As seen in the above section, Argentina, Brazil, and Chile have important incentives for increasing their political and security cooperation. Nevertheless, as Jaguaribe correctly underlined, "the international meaning of Mercosur depends on reaching an internal consensus regarding the countries' foreign policies" (1998: 145). However, this foreign policy consensus has been complicated by the countries' contending visions about the goal security cooperation should pursue, their relations with the United States, and even the scope of their security interests.

### 1. Argentina: Two Contradictory Strategic Alliances.

For many observers of the region, the main problem for increased security cooperation has been the Argentine alignment with the United States during the 1990s, which has been a new strategic reality within the region.

Argentina's change had a basic and very visible rationale: the new economic model demanded an adequate relationship with the political and economic center, but the country was internationally isolated after a long history of international behavior that had systematically confronted Washington. Menem's government pushed a radical and even apparently exaggerated shift toward a full and explicit bandwagoning with the U.S., and foreign policy became "a calculated acquiescence to the political needs of the United States and other Western powers", oriented to be "perceived as functional to the generators of positive perceptions among financiers and potential investors" (Escudé 1998: 53, 55). The policy was systematically followed by the Menem administration. In 1997, the U.S. granted the country the status of Non-NATO Major Ally (Saín 1999: 143), which was seen by Chile (and Brazil) as "a new element in the always delicate existing regional balances in the Southern Cone" (Van Klaveren 1997: 37).

Therefore, Argentina's international success was related to its capacity to simultaneously articulate a two-pillared strategy: to develop Mercosur's project, but also to both successfully engage and subordinate itself to the global and regional U.S. agenda, especially in political (human rights) and security affairs (peace operations under Chapter VII of the U.N. Charter in which the U.S. has special interests at stake) (Escudé and Fontana 1998, Lagorio 1998). The implications of this two-pillared strategy are relevant for this thesis: as Escudé explained, behind this apparent contradiction, the "chosen mechanism is one of two complementary alliances with each one counterbalancing the other", a policy "dictated by one value: the promotion of the economic welfare" of the Argentine people (Escudé, 1999: 86).

However, at the same time, the Argentine rapprochement with the United States has an additional rationale, closer to her strategic self-perception within the Southern Cone. Despite the formal elimination of traditional conflict hypothesis with Brazil and the rhetorical Argentine-Brazilian commitments to build a "strategic alliance" (Mercosur 1997), the relationship with the United States was useful for Buenos Aires to reduce the Brazilian hegemony during the complex process toward further integration, and also to ameliorate the pressure from the Chilean and British (Malvinas/Falklands) sides. As Bouzas pointed out, for Argentina the rapprochement with Chile has meant access for its products to the Pacific ports, but also has served to build "a critical mass to counterbalance Brazil's weight and influence in Mercosur", especially because Santiago and Buenos Aires share a common approach regarding the FTAA negotiations. They want to accelerate the process not only as a strategy to increase their markets, but also, especially for Argentina, the FTAA is an indirect way of pushing the opening of the still highly protected Brazilian market. Equally relevant, and maybe even more sensitive for Buenos Aires, in addition to the issue of Brazil, during the 1990s Chile formally began to support Argentine sovereignty claims over the Malvinas/Falkland Islands in the context of Menem's non-military strategy in the international forums, particularly at the UN, an issue frequently forgotten in the international analysis. That is, the strategic rapprochement with Chile also helped Argentina to weaken the British position regarding the South Atlantic area.

On the whole, Argentina has managed its foreign policy with ability during the 1990s structuring a network with the US., Brazil, and Chile aiming at simultaneous goals: to mitigate Brazilian hegemony within the integration process, to compensate eventual military imbalances with Chile (Escudé and Fontana 1998: 63-5), to reduce British maneuvering room in relation to the U.S. regarding the Malvinas/Falkland question, and --essentially--to strengthen its international and sub-regional economic insertion and its domestic welfare.

Compared with Brazil and Chile, Argentina has been the most interested in further advances toward sub-regional security and military cooperation because such advances are functional for strengthening all of her new strategic alliances with the U.S., Brazil, and even Chile. High-level Argentine officials and officers have sketched ideas about a "small-NATO" within Mercosur (Pion-Berlin 2000: 50-1), and several steps have been taken in this direction, especially since the 1997 Argentine-Brazilian institution of the Permanent Mechanism for Consultation and Coordination. In contrast to Brazilian authorities, who were more cautious on the implications of the agreement, Diego Guelar, the Argentine ambassador to Brazil stated that the Mechanism "will be a defense scheme from Amazon to Antarctica". In addition, Argentine Deputy Foreign Affairs Minister Andrés Cisneros explained that this initiative corresponded to a "second phase" of the Argentine-Brazilian rapprochement, the first being the 1985 nuclear agreements, and the second, the establishment of the customs union (Clarín 1997). This second phase has been reflected in domestic Argentine adjustments in the defense sector.

On July 28, 1997 the Undersecretary of Military Affairs of the Ministry of Defense prepared the working paper "Common Security System". It proposed a crisis prevention mechanism for Mercosur based on "the intervention of the armed forces to determine, prevent, and discourage processes of social, cultural and/or political destabilization within the member states, and to 'prevent and discourage eventual clandestine armed groups' and 'violence eruptions' originated in 'indigenism, peasants, subversion, terrorism, drug trafficking, etcetera'" (Saín 1999: 154).

In 1998 Argentina promulgated the "Law of Military Restructuring". Article 6 establishes that "the restructuring will consider the employment of the military instrument" to support "friendly countries", while Article 7 added that "the levels of strategic conduction and strategic planning will analyze, at international level, the probable development of a defense system within the framework of Mercosur, to the ends of considering in the Armed Forces restructuring the requirements that may emerge from those agreements" (Diamint 1998: 65).

Therefore, Argentina is willing to advance toward further sub-regional regimes of security cooperation, but her foreign policy is also subordinated to the strategic alliance with the U.S.

## 2. Brazil: Between Autonomy and Subordination to Mercosur's Discipline.

Contrary to Argentina, Brazil envisions sub-regional cooperation whose main goal is to enhance her international autonomy, which has originated a more distant relationship with the United States, and sees with distrust cooperative schemes that could tend to increase Washington's hegemony in the region. Much of this quest for autonomy comes from Brazil's self-perception as an actor of global dimensions with interests of global scope (Guedes Da Costa 2000: 21, Costa 1999: 89-106), but also from the logic that because its economy is still highly protected, especially its highly developed industrial and financial sectors, is a country that still has much to protect against U.S. pressures for fast liberalization, and therefore needs strategic capacity to back this posture[103].

The Brazilian quest for higher autonomy than Argentina has not meant bad relationships with the U.S. After the 1980s, the U.S. became, as it was for Argentina, crucial for the success of Brazil, especially for the reconstruction of its damaged financial reputation after the debt crisis (Guedes Da Costa 2000: 22). The rapprochement with

---

[103] Brazilian globalism, however, has transitioned among different meanings since World War II. Before the end of the bureaucratic authoritarian regime (1964-1985) the country developed strategic capabilities, including the nuclear and missile programs as well as the nuclear-propelled submarines. Although these were aimed not to confront major powers but to counterbalance the Argentine nuclear build-up initiated in the 1950s (Jones et. Al. 1998: 231), Brazilian "peripheral autonomy" (the concept coined by Helio Jaguaribe in 1975) gave the country *de facto* credentials as a global player (Costa 1999: 95), beginning a period of deterioration in bilateral relations with the United States. Open contestation of U.S. attempts to curb Brazilian strategic programs was later complicated by the distance that Washington adopted from Southern Cone military regimes despite its initial support for the national security regimes (Stepan 1973, Fitch 1994).

Argentina became very helpful in this respect, ending the Brazilian nuclear program and its adherence to the Missile Technology Control Regime (MTCR), which eased its relationships with Washington. However, several issues remained to generate further frictions, especially those related to the mastering of nuclear and space technologies and, in general, high-tech sectors, where Brazil pursues a relatively independent policy with the most technologically advanced Third World countries, particularly with China, India and South Africa. In Brazilian perceptions, this area remains crucial for the country not only because of its strategic implications but also because of economic strategic considerations. The Brazilian economic strategy is based on the transformation of its huge industrial sector toward one that is more knowledge-based and, thus, more internationally competitive under globalization conditions (Guedes Da Costa 1998: 55). However, this effort is perceived as having been deliberately restricted by the "cartel of knowledge" (Vieira 1994).

Differences with the U.S. have also been also nurtured by diverging views about the post-Cold War reform of the international system. Brazil has favored more democratic international security institutions, demanding the regulation of the veto power of permanent members of the U.N. Security Council and the enlargement of the Council, proclaiming its candidacy as representative of Latin America. It has also opposed the great powers' trend toward increasing intervention during the post-Cold War era. In relation to international trade, Brazil supports the process of liberalization within the WTO but favors moderate approaches and paces, more attuned to countries like herself, with long processes of economic transformation, while the U.S., better positioned to compete under more deregulated markets, has pressed for a more aggressive liberalization; this difference is also reflected in the contending approaches the two countries have regarding the FTAA.

Within this context, Brazil has assumed the emergence of Mercosur as a valuable strategy to strengthen its policy of international autonomy, especially regarding the U.S.[104], and, within this framework, several members of the Brazilian elite clearly favor the adoption of a Mercosur strategic dimension, assuming that its role as international actor would be strengthened if Mercosur had a common or joint defense policy (Escudé and Fontana 1998: 70-6)[105]. Military chiefs have favored the development of a Mercosur collective defense, but aiming to address Brazilian concerns about the strategic implications of an eventual foreign hegemonic intervention in South America (Vieira 1994). However, given the Argentine strategic rapprochement with the U.S., Mercosur's collective defense seems unviable. It is important to highlight that the Brazilian quest for autonomy undermines its relationships not only with the United States, but even with Argentina, Paraguay, and Uruguay. Mercosur must be understood as an important strategy for Brazil to the extent that it respects the moderate pace of the Brazilian process of re-industrialization. However (and as will be seen below in part C of this Chapter), when Brazilian authorities think Mercosur may produce higher costs than gains, they usually cheat. This behavior has been possible because of the extreme economic

---

[104] In the most extreme versions, part of the Brazilian elite expects Mercosur to be part of the "World Directorate" if a multipolar international system arises in the next decades (Jaguaribe 1998). However, more moderated approaches have prevailed, especially during Cardoso's government (Escudé and Fontana 1998: 72).

[105] Escudé and Fontana quote an intervention by Helio Jaguaribe in 1994 to sustain this assertion. However, in a more recent work, Jaguaribe makes an important distinction, explaining that according to his view, the consolidation of Mercosur as an international actor must not necessarily be understood as a confrontational strategy regarding the United States. He considers that if the world system is finally articulated upon the U.S. imperial order, the members of Mercosur will be in a better position to negotiate its adherence to such an imperial pole than through isolated, FTAA-type strategies (Jaguaribe 1998: 145-7).

asymmetry between Brazil and the rest of the group (about 80 percent of its combined GDP), and the still relatively secondary (although important) relevance of Mercosur for its exports (22 percent as against 38 percent in the Argentine case in 1999). Therefore, the Brazilian search for autonomy is not mechanically convergent with the development of Mercosur.

Finally, from a geostrategic point of view, Brazilian priorities are not the same as those of Argentina and Chile. Its strategic interests has been described according to the logic of concentric rings in which the most peripheral corresponds to the international security agenda as discussed above. A second ring would be the immediate perimeter: the management of the Amazon and Plata basins (with all the state and non-state actors acting in this area), and the South Atlantic (where 90 percent of Brazilian foreign trade flows). Thus, from a strategic point of view "the concept of the 'Southern Cone' is too narrow for Brazilian strategists who take a broader view of the country's perimeter, a fact reinforced by the Brazilian perception of nonexistence of military threats from neighboring countries and its unreachable strategic superiority" (Guedes Da Costa 1998: 53). As Pion-Berlin has noted (2000: 52-3), the more pressing threats to Brazilian security are closer to its northern border, related to border transgressions resulting from drug trafficking, terrorism, and immigration, and consequently are problems preferably to be resolved with countries around the Amazon basin (Peru, Ecuador, Colombia, Venezuela, and Guyana), but not with the Mercosur countries or Chile. In this context Southern Cone strategic issues have played a secondary role in Brazilian foreign policy during the 1990s, and despite the rapprochement with Argentina, beyond bilateral regimes, Brazilian strategic goals regarding Mercosur are less clear and more diffuse.

### 3. Chile. Seeking Autonomy and Political Leverage. Are Both Possible?

The articulation between its global interests and the integration process during the 1990s put Chile into an intermediate position between Argentina and Brazil. Chile's foreign and security policies during the 1990s have expressed the diversification of its national interests as a consequence of its highly diversified trade pattern, which in turn led to a more balanced approach in strategic affairs. However, the country did not find a precise correlation between this "multiple economic insertion" and any strategic option (Ministerio de Defensa Nacional 1997: 42). Instead of that, Chile opted for balanced and positive, but autonomous, relationships with the U.S., the European Union, Latin America, and the Asia-Pacific, and an increased profile in the UN security agenda and multilateral forums.

At the international level Chile has converged with Brazil in promoting a reformed U.N. Security Council. However, Santiago has opposed Brazil's pretension of becoming the region's representative, advocating an alternative rotating representative to be elected among the Latin American countries. Also like Brazil, Chile has criticized the great powers' increasing post-Cold War interventionism, but has adopted an intermediate position. In 1999, after the Kosovo crisis and a decade of increasing its participation in peacekeeping operations (Ministerio de Defensa Nacional 1997), the Chilean government decided to support U.N.-regulated humanitarian intervention. As in the Argentine case, this was a shift from its traditional, Latin American-centered foreign policy of non-intervention. However, it was carried out without abandoning Chile's opposition to U.S. unilateral use of force in the region (Fernández 2001).

At the hemispheric level, and because of its radical economic liberalization and the restoration of the democratic regime, in 1990 Chile was willing to restore a positive relationship with the U.S. Its immediate goal was direct entrance into NAFTA in 1994[106], and both Santiago and Washington also had strategic interests in the normalization of their military relationships after the military government (Varas and Fuentes 1994: 110). In 1990 Chile secured the end of the 1977 Kennedy-Hartman Amendment, while the U.S. began to reverse the "decline" of its military influence (Fitch 1994) in an important Latin American player. In this sense, Chilean economic policies led to strong divergences with Brazil but proximity with Argentina because Chile was unwilling to submit its economic strategy to the interminable Brazilian-U.S. economic negotiation.

However, like Brazil's, Chile's search for autonomy led to friction with Washington regarding the U.S. attempts during the early 1990s to impose "new roles and missions" for the armed forces (drug enforcement and peacekeeping and peace enforcement operations). The U.S. policies were perceived as risky because Chile still had territorial defense at the top of its strategic agenda. This framework also conditioned the perception of the 1995 U.S. proposals of new hemispheric "cooperative security" policies, especially when they converged with Argentine proposals toward sub-regional military integration through a collective alliance (Escudé 1998: 61, Pion-Berlin 2000: 50). In turn, the already mentioned new status granted to Argentina as Non-NATO Major Ally, affected Chile's disposition against Argentina's Southern Cone proposals of security integration, since they could imply increased degrees of U.S. hegemony but also

---

[106] From a Chilean perspective, Van Klaveren offers an excellent summary of U.S.-Chilean relations during the 1990s (1997: 135-8). For analysis of previous decades centered on the strategic variables, see Meneses 1989, 1993.

extreme imbalances in relation to Argentina. Contrary to Argentina, Chile did not needed to bandwagon. In contrast with Argentina, Chile was not in a double, internal and external, critical position at the beginning of its new democratic period. Unlike to most of the Latin American countries, Chile had scheduled and honored its structural adjustment programs with the IMF during the late 1980s, and when democracy was restored in 1990 the country was in the early phase of a long cycle of economic growth and in a particularly propitious position in its relationships with the international financial institutions.

In the end, the Chilean balance regarding the more political and strategic implications of Mercosur have been mixed. If the Chilean government has been conscious of the limits of Mercosur for Chile's immediate economic interests, at the same time, it has demonstrated an increasing sensitivity to the political and strategic effects of the consolidation of Mercosur as a mechanism of political concertation. This dimension of the Chilean foreign policy is relatively new, but it has been clearly expressed since 1996. According to the Chilean Foreign Affairs Minister, "it is in the fundamental interest for Chile to create the conditions" for Chilean accession to Mercosur, because "it is a strategic project" aimed to "face globalization" by forming a "powerful block which should have not only commercial characteristics, but also political and social" ones (Ministerio de Relaciones Exteriores 2000c, 2000f). Within this context, and despite the unresolved economic divergences, in 1997 Chile formally requested (and Mercosur accepted) its incorporation into the institutional structures of the group, the Consultation and Political Concertation Mechanism of Mercosur, which was formalized by Mercosur's Decisión 12/97. Thus, Chile and Mercosur advanced from a free trade area "toward an association of political and strategic[107] character" (Ministerio de Relaciones Exteriores 2001d). The 1997 agreement was later confirmed and deepened during the June 2000 Mercosur Presidential Summit in Buenos Aires (June), when the chiefs of state agreed to begin formal negotiations aiming at the full incorporation of Chile in the group[108], but the talks were suspended in the next meeting at Florianapolis (December) after Chile and the U.S. announced the beginning of their negotiations regarding a bilateral free trade agreement.

In strategic terms, Chilean policies regarding further cooperation within the Southern Cone have been, again, different from those advanced by Argentina and Brazil. Beyond the initial goal of stabilizing and securing the new economic interdependence with Argentina and the Southern Cone seen in Chapter III, Chile has informally proposed to increase security cooperation through multilateral cooperation in the Southern Cone. Three arguments have been deployed favoring this alternative.

First, there is a growing Chilean interest in Southern Cone security cooperation regarding an agenda that Santiago perceives as transnational and regional in scope in that can be addressed only through intergovernmental coordination. The agenda is related to the protection of the environment, especially from risky and predatory management by external powers, and of territorial integrity regarding the growing concentration of land ownership by foreign (American) investors in unpopulated areas of the Chilean and Argentine southern regions (Pérez 1997). The Chilean approach has received initial support from Argentina, and bilateral naval cooperation has began aiming to control the

---

[107] Note of the author: "strategic" in relation to the political and economic goals, not military.

[108] According to the chief Chilean negotiator with Mercosur, the preliminary negotiations were initially expected to be completed in 2002 (Rosales 2000: 1).

transport of radioactive material through southern waters and the conservation of the Antarctic waters. However, the evolution of the Chilean proposals from bilateral toward some form of sub-regional cooperative regimes will depend on how important Brazil perceives its maritime and Antarctic interests to be, or on how well these environmental security dimensions, located in the region's geographical extremes, can be regionally articulated[109]. In addition, the military dimension of environmental cooperation within the Southern Cone will probably be carefully managed if disputes arise (for instance, around the fisheries, as they usually do in the region[110]); they will be also cautiously managed because they usually involve clashes with powers that are also crucial economic and political partners in other areas, especially the European Union and Japan[111].

Second, the Chilean defense paper also made an ambiguous but suggestive assertion. On the one hand, it expressed a clear preference for sub-regional security regimes, promoting "continental coordination, preferably by specific geographic areas, to prevent crisis and to maintain peace, instead of the design of new global schemes of collective security", and also stated that "a solid economic complementation favors some political integration, which could make it convenient to design a military mechanism for regional cooperation, if not against external threats to the conglomerate of integrated

[109] For instance, in April 2001, acting on behalf of the Río Group, the Chilean Foreign Affairs Ministry deplored the U.S. withdrawal from the Kyoto regime for gas emissions. However, Mercosur has not yet advanced with political initiatives in the environmental area. See Ministerio de Relaciones Exteriores 2001e.

[110] Maritime incidents within the EEZ and territorial waters are frequent between Southern Cone states and European factory ships. For instance, on December 2000 the World Trade Organization accepted a European Union request to establish a panel to solve its dispute with Chile around swordfish captures. Chile accepted the panel, but prefers to address the conflict within the framework of the U.N. Convention on International Sea Law. See Ministerio de Relaciones Exteriores 2000e.

[111] The main conflicts between Southern Cone countries and Japan revolve around the transport of radioactive material for the Japanese nuclear-powered energy industry and the protection of some important species in danger of extinction, such as whales.

countries, with the purpose of providing it with support and credibility in any negotiation between blocks" (Libro de la Defensa Nacional 1997:58-9). The implications of this approach are still unclear, but it seems to be opening the way for increasing Chilean participation if Mercosur finally is consolidated as a political instance.

Third, the diversification of Chilean economic interests resulting from its diversified market pattern (90 percent of its trade, accounting for almost 40 percent of its GDP, currently flows through the seas) has given the country a more cosmopolitan scope of security policies. Therefore, defense policies have been adapted to a more active involvement in United Nations coalitional efforts to maintain stability, but integration is perceived as a privileged space in which to develop converging security policies.

Therefore, sub-regional economic integration and market diversification are acting as complementary forces prompting security cooperation in the Southern Cone. As the Chilean Navy chief stated in 1999, because the "integration process will advance and will be consolidated [...], this reality puts before us the necessity to visualize paths to advance toward the design of doctrines and the attainment of equipment to allow the inter-operability of our naval forces. These measures are not an end in themselves, but prior and indispensable actions to reach the capacity to combine our forces when necessary and convenient for the protection of the interests of the international and regional" community (Arancibia 1999). Consequently, the first practical steps in this direction have begun between Chile and Argentina. As noted in Chapter III, the two countries initiated in 1999 their joint Antarctic patrols, which involve increasing standardization in communications and interoperability.

In sum, Chile sees powerful incentives to increase its security cooperation with Argentina and Brazil, but the strategic relationships with these two countries are complex and contradictory.

## 4. Conclusions.

Given the alternatives of emerging security cooperation at the sub-regional level, and potential emergence of regimes around the idea of some type of collective action at the international level, it is worth noting that all the alternatives imply the development of higher levels of military interoperability, and that military cooperation aiming at increased interoperability is already ongoing bilaterally between Argentina and Brazil and between Argentina and Chile, as well as in the context of the military exercises fostered by the U.S. Southern Command[112]. Moreover, Argentine and Chilean civilian authorities (Pérez 1997, La Nación 2001b[113]) and military officers (Vieira 1994, Balza 1995, Arancibia 1999) have publicly expressed a positive disposition toward at least sub-regional multilateral security cooperation.

The constraints on increased Southern Cone security and military cooperation are, however, also important. Brazil and Chile distrust Argentine proposals for sub-regional military forces[114], and for both countries the Argentine quasi-alliance with the United

---

[112] The main peacekeeping military multilateral exercises promoted by the U.S. in the region are the "Cabañas". See U.S. Southern Command (2000).

[113] The last Argentine proposition regarding increasing security cooperation was formulated by the Minister of Defense, Horacio Jaunarena, in April 2001, a few days after his appointment. Jaunarena advocated a more moderated path, beginning with an "office of strategic reflection at the Mercosur level, including Chile and Bolivia", and did not reject the possibility of a joint staff of Mercosur. See La Nación 2001b.

[114] Brazilian and Chilean (and other Latin American) distrust of some type of multinational sub-regional military force is based on fears of U.S. manipulation behind Argentine initiatives. While Argentina has proposed Mercosur multinational military forces explicitly aimed to intervene in the region, the U.S. has explored the regional reception for a multilateral intervention to defend democratic regimes, but has carefully avoided explicit references to its eventual armed character. For U.S. proposals see Marrero 1999.

139

States has been a perturbing fact. In relation to Brazil, Chile's more immediate military strategic interests tend to be concentrated on its perimeter (Argentina, Bolivia, Peru, the Southern Pacific, and Antarctica), which makes cooperation more plausible with Argentina but too peripheral for Brazilian interests. This dispersion of security interests may diminish incentives for cooperation.

Furthermore, security cooperation does not mean not to deter. Deterrence remains the basic behavior between Argentina and Chile and, to some extent, for Argentina regarding Brazil[115]. But as seen in Chapter III, countries like Argentina and Chile seem to be able to overcome or deliberately ignore the problem of balance if it remains within acceptable margins, and if gains from increased cooperation are bigger that losses from partial changes in balance.

Deterrence will continue to endure because arms control agreements have proved difficult to negotiate as the result of the scope of the strategic interests of the three different countries. The Brazilian scope includes but is not limited to Mercosur and is to some extent insensitive to Argentine strategic concerns (Guedes Da Costa 1998). And the Argentine and Chilean scope are both regional and global, thus demanding a military apparatus credible enough both to produce deterrence at the immediate (but extensive-- territorial, aerial and naval) perimeter of their defense, and also to project some minimal level of force to serve their limited but global interests.

---

For a critical assessment of Marrero's proposal in the context of the Colombian crisis, see Stratfor.com 1999.

[115] In the same article, Jaunarena stated that "the conflicts with Brazil and Chile are practically discarded or, at least, they are diminished in a big way". La Nación 2001a.

## C. ECONOMIC INTEGRATION: THE CRISIS OF THE CUSTOMS UNION, AND THE FREEZING OF CHILEAN ACCESS.

The basic condition for the consolidation of Mercosur as a forum of political concertation and, therefore, as an actor of regional dimensions in the international system is the strengthening of the customs union. This is the basis for its agenda of international negotiations with other groups and powers, and without it there is no rationale for its differentiation as the core inner ring within the Rio Group and for the development of a distinctive, common foreign security policy.

However, since its creation in 1991 the group has evidenced a highly contradictory economic process characterized by increasing economic interdependence, and even gradual macroeconomic economic convergence, but also by growing economic conflicts originating in the countries' different degrees of interdependence and economic asymmetry, but also in different rhythms of national economic liberalization, which dictate different policies in economic areas that are critical under conditions of high interdependence.

This section will analyze the advance of the process of economic integration (and not only the increase of interdependence as Chapter III did) to obtain a more nuanced assessment of the political and strategic prospects of Mercosur, particularly regarding the possibility of further political and security cooperation. This will be done through a study of the evolution of the goals that the Treaty of Asunción instituted: the free trade area, the establishment of a customs union, and the coordination of macroeconomic policies and harmonization of domestic legislation in sectors relevant to integration.

## 1. The Sub-Regional Free Market Zone[116]: Reached but Conflictive.

The Asunción Treaty established an automatic, progressive, and linear reduction of all tariffs and the elimination of non-tariff and similar barriers to attain zero tariff, as well as the total elimination of other barriers to intra-Mercosur trade by December 31 1994. Although more than 90 percent of tariffs were included in the program, a list of exceptions (some of them very important within Mercosur economies, such as the car and sugar industries) was adopted, along with special regimes applying to sensitive industries. In 1994 the Protocol of Ouro Preto established a 10-year delay for the elimination of exceptions and special regimes. Paraguay and Uruguay were given longer delays, a slower progression of tariff reduction and longer lists of exceptions. Since then, evolution of the free trade zone has been as shown in Table 4:

---

[116] This part draws basically from the Inter American Development Bank (IADB) Periodic Notes and the IADB Country Economic Assessment Reports (Averbug 2000, Dinsmoor 2000, and Quintero 2000).

| Issue | Advances |
|---|---|
| Tariffs | Most intra-regional tariffs were dismantled according to the agreed timetable, with the majority of intra-regional trade facing zero duties since 1995. |
| Exceptions | Some sensitive goods were initially excluded from the free trade area, but have been incorporated after several conflicts. The most important cases have been the car industry, on which the group reached an agreement only in 2000, and sugar on which no agreement has been possible. |
| Non-tariffs | • **Brazil** unilaterally established a new system of customs valuation. In December 1997, it imposed a system of discretionary licenses for a number of imports including dairy products, fuels, fruits, certain chemicals and machinery, and restrictions on some of the affected items were further increased in 1998[117].<br>• **Argentina** adopted its own import restrictions, including a regime for pre-shipment inspection of most imported consumer goods, introduced in March 1999. Argentine trade authorities have also called for a discussion of safeguard arrangements (there are none in Mercosur), import quotas and new tariffs to protect domestic industries from sudden surges in imports from other Mercosur countries (restrictions would cover shoes, aluminum, some textile products and some laminated steel). Argentina has abstained from actually implementing such measures in view of disagreement among its trade partners.<br>Countries have introduced a number of **regulatory and administrative practices** seemingly aimed at curbing or delaying imports.<br>• Brazil introduced limits to the financing of imports in late 1997 and new measures to control product quality, dumping and under-invoicing in September 1998.<br>• Uruguay resorted to tight enforcement of inspection in cross-border trade.<br>Argentina introduced new import quotas for textile and clothing products and anti-dumping duties on steel laminates imported from all sources in July 1999. Two months later, Brazil responded by announcing restrictions on 400 Argentine products (food products, textiles and footwear). Argentina, in turn, announced non-automatic import licenses on paper from all sources, including Brazil, reinforcing labeling requirements imposed a week earlier. In the end of September, Argentine and Brazilian manufacturers of footwear and paper products agreed to quantitative limits on Brazilian exports to Argentina. This agreement has reduced the level of trade tension between the two countries. Meanwhile, Brazil has refrained from applying the restrictions on 400 Argentine products (IADB 1999: 26-7). |

Table 4. Evolution of Mercosur Free Trade Zone.

As is observable, the assessment of the creation of the free trade area is positive, but also involves some hostility and a conflictive relationship.

---

[117] The resulting conflict led to the formation of a three-member tribunal to resolve the dispute. The tribunal ruled the regime should be dismantled by the end of 1999. This was the first time that Mercosur's countries had used their dispute settlement mechanism since the approval of the Brasilia Protocol in 1994. In the past, differences had mostly settled through bilateral agreements among the parties at high diplomatic levels.

## 2. The Progressive Crisis of the Customs Union.

The Protocol of Ouro Preto downgraded the full-fledged common market, to be completed by 1995, into a customs union. The external tariffs of the four countries were then converted to a common level, averaging the higher Brazilian tariffs and the lower tariffs of the three other countries, which meant the 1995 introduction of a "common external tariff (CET) structure ranging from zero to 20 percent" for approximately 85 percent of the goods, and a simple average Most Favored Nation (MFN) tariff for the trade block declining from 41 percent in 1986 to 14 percent in 1997 (IADSB 1999: 24-5, Devlin et al 1999: 4). A ten-year transition period was adopted to eliminate exceptions, and new exceptions would apply pending consultation among the four countries. Since then, as Figure 18 shows, the CET has been applied. However, it has not been fully implemented, and has suffered strong blows that progressively threaten its continuation.

A first set of exceptions to the CET were negotiated among Mercosur's governments:

- Fifteen percent of sensitive goods not included in the CET were excluded from the free trade area until December 1999. Also, capital goods, computers and related software, and telecommunications equipment are not yet included in the CET regime. Each Mercosur country is presently allowed to charge its own tariff rate on these goods. For capital goods, tariff rates should converge at 14 percent by January 2001 for Argentina and Brazil, and by January 2006 for Paraguay and Uruguay. In the case of computers and related software and telecommunications equipment, tariff rates must converge at 16 percent for all countries by 2006 (IADB 1999: 25).

- In November 1997, following the onset of the international financial crisis, the Mercosur Council approved an Argentine proposal to raise the CET by 3 points until December 31, 2000. Argentina and Brazil adopted this new measure, while Paraguay and Uruguay expressed strong reservations about implementing it in full and, to date, have applied it only selectively. Brazil increased import duties on several products in mid-1998 in an effort to prevent a further widening of its current account deficit (IADB 1999: 26).

A second source of violations of the CET have been countries' unilateral decisions:

- In 1995, as a consequence of the Mexican financial crisis, Argentina "temporarily" restored the "statistical tax" of 3 percent on non-Mercosur imports.

- In April 1995, Brazil raised tariffs on 109 products from 32 percent to 70 percent, and quotas were established on automobile imports. To curb inflation, the list of exceptions to the CET was increased from 350 to 450 products.

- Also, the integrity of the CET regime (and of Mercosur as a political forum of concertation) and, hence, the consolidation of the customs union in 2006 has been compromised by a number of recent bilateral agreements signed between individual Mercosur countries and third parties. Argentina and Mexico signed a trade accord in 1998, while Brazil unilaterally advanced with the Andean Community.

- However, the most important CET crisis arose in March 2001, when the new Minister of Economy, Domingo Cavallo, announced the unilateral Argentine abolition of tariffs for capital equipment, and raised those for consumer goods to the maximum established by the Asunción and Ouro Preto treaties, 35 percent (The Economist 2001). This led Brazilian authorities to acknowledge that, in effect, Mercosur's customs union had been "suspended", although "only temporarily" (The Economist 2001:33, El Mercurio 2001a).

### 3. Macroeconomic Policies. Structural Differences But Partial Convergence.

The Treaties of Asunción and Ouro Preto did not create formal mechanisms of coordination, which it was agreed would proceed based on informal intergovernmental coordination. However, this regime has functioned with another feature: informal consultation has operated *ex post*. In practice, the group has not developed any type of macroeconomic convergence, but it has resulted nevertheless because of the similarities of the different domestic processes of economic liberalization. Some indicators will be

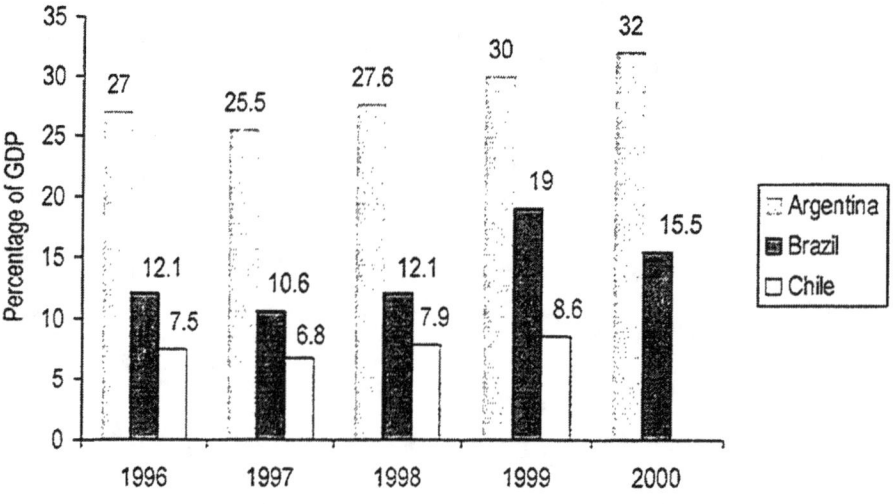

Figure 22. Public Debt As % of GDP.

*(Source: author upon IMF 2000, 2000a, 2000b[119])*

---

[119] Chilean data for 2000 is not available in IMF's source.

It is clear that the three countries are converging in terms of inflation and interest rates, and even in terms of public debt they have a growing but still manageable standard[120]. However, the exchange rate policy has been the most difficult policy area. Argentina opted for fixed exchange to the US dollar while Chile and Brazil had mixed regimes of controlled floatation that were replaced in 1997 and 1999, respectively, by free floating as strategies to improve their exports, trade balances, public deficits and current accounts. Since 1994 Brazil has made four substantial and non-consulted devaluations, the last one, adopted in January 1999 (43.9 percent), to address the effects of the Asian financial crisis and the increasing Brazilian trade deficit. But a more complete picture of the problem, especially for Argentina, has been the combination of the Chilean and Brazilian devaluations between 1990-2000, shown in Figure 23 and Figure 24.

Because the Brazilian and Chilean markets account for more than 36 percent of Argentine exports, their policies severely damaged external Argentine competitiveness, reducing the national revenues for both the private and public Argentine sectors. The Brazilian devaluation has been seen as the main (although not the only) factor producing a 20 percent fall in the bilateral trade and the worst Argentine recession since the 1980s.

---

[120] It is worth noting that the European criterion regarding public debt for the Economic Union in 1999 was 60 percent of GDP (McCormick 1999: 196).

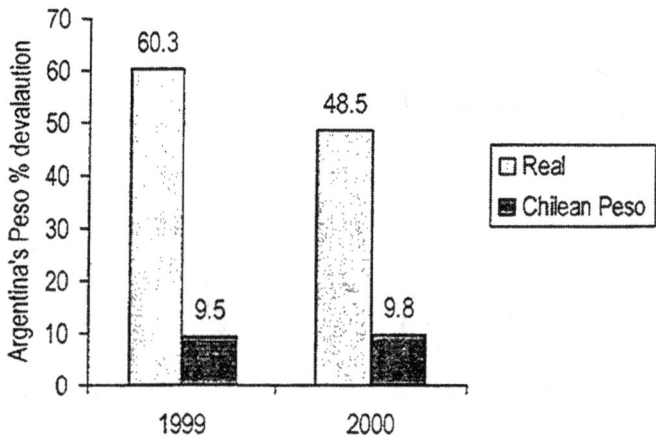

Figure 24. Brazilian and Chilean Devaluation Regarding Argentina's Peso.

*(Source: author, based upon ECLAC 2000)*

---

[121] The average of the indices for the real (main official) exchange rate for the currency of each country against the currencies of its main trading partners, weighted according to the relative magnitude of imports from these countries. The weights reflect the average for the 1994-1998 period.

The net outcome of the 1999-2000 economic crisis has been the entrance of Mercosur into a critical period, with serious possibilities of governments abandoning it. According to several non-official and independent reports, President Cardoso and Minister Luiz Felipe Lampreia privately considered this alternative at the and of 1999 (América Economía 2000a). The just-appointed Minister of Economy Domingo Cavallo not only "temporarily" dragged Argentina out of the customs union in March 2001, but in April 2001 he passed a new law initiating the end of dollarization and the adoption of a mixed exchange regime (the peso's "convertibility", that is, its peg to a basket composed of the dollar and the euro, with the possibility of being extended to the yen), beginning a gradual transition toward a more competitive currency, trying to apply this shift with the lowest political cost possible[122]. However, the possibility of permanently leaving the customs union was not completely discarded[123].

After this critical period, there appear to be at least four main requisites for the continuation of the economic integration: the maintenance of market liberalization processes, deeper macroeconomic convergence, particularly a stronger Brazilian commitment to trade liberalization, and a change in the Argentine exchange policy. These two last two shifts, in turn, could facilitate Chile's full accession to the group, which could accelerate Mercosur's trade and economic diversification in the Asia-Pacific, a

---

[122] On April 15, 2001, Minister of Economy Domingo Cavallo did send to the legislature a bill that would end the Argentine peso's 10-year-old one-to-one peg to the dollar, attaching the currency instead to a 50-50 average of the dollar and the euro and, eventually, the yen. The move would not take place until the values of the dollar and euro reached parity. The new exchange policy continues a fixed exchange regime but opens the way for a transition to a controlled or free floating. See The New York Times 2001, 2001a.

[123] During the Third Summit of the Americas at Quebec City, Canada, in April 2001, Cavallo declared that he was personally willing to break ranks with Mercosur. "I have my point of view but now I'm minister of the Economy so I'm an obedient member of the government of [President Fernando] De La Rúa. For the moment, we are only going to negotiate through Mercosur". See Financial Times 2001.

development that would be critical if Argentina wanted to reduce her dependence on Brazil. Not surprisingly, during 2000 and 2001 Argentina and Brazil (and Mercosur) adopted some initial steps in the direction of the above-mentioned four policy requisites.

First, all the countries have continued their domestic processes of market liberalization (ECLAC 2000). Second, during 2000 Mercosur made a number of important strides towards the establishment of an effective policy coordination system, publicly presenting it as its "relaunching". The most important agreement[124] was the institutionalization of a macroeconomic oversight group formed by experts from the four Mercosur member States and its associates (Bolivia and Chile) whose mandate was to prepare a macroeconomic convergence program of economic targets to enter into effect in 2001 and cover the years up to 2010, aiming to consolidate the customs union and prepare the monetary union. The package was approved by the countries at the Florianopolis (Brazil) Summit meeting of the Common Market Council in December 2001, and its goals include inflation (an annual 5% per annum between 2002 and 2005 and no more than 4% starting in 2006), fiscal debt (no more than 3% of GDP in 2002), and public debt (maximum 40% of GDP by 2010). With a view to this objective, triennial transitional goals have been established and a ceiling has been set for the consolidated public-sector deficit equivalent to 3% of GDP in 2002, although Brazil is authorized to reach 3.5% in 2002 and 2003 (El Mercurio 2000b). The governments also agreed to increase convergence in macroeconomic management, which was backed by the first Argentine moves toward a more flexible exchange rate, while Brazil agreed to make its

---

[124] At the meeting the countries' authorities also agreed to increase their macroeconomic coordination and convergence as crucial to the association's future, and acknowledged the need to make certain that their various exchange-rate regimes were compatible so that they could achieve a genuine form of macroeconomic coordination and convergence and thus ensure fiscal sustainability and price stability.

152

posture flexible regarding the FTAA during the Third Summit of the Americas at Quebec, Canada, in April 2001. During this meeting Brazil agreed to conclude the FTAA negotiations "no latter than 2005 and to seek its entry into force as soon as possible thereafter, but in any case, no later than December 2005" (SAIN 2001), shifting from its original position of beginning FTAA negotiations by 2005[125]. Both continuing market liberalization and increased policy coordination were important, providing a certain credibility to the agreement on macroeconomic convergence within the context of the Argentine-Brazilian bilateral economic crisis.

Therefore, as previously seen, economic integration has been both positive and negative for the interests of the Southern Cone countries. Moreover, its importance has varied according to the relative magnitude of the intra-regional interdependence of each state.

Argentina has been both the most favored because the increase of her exports, and the most damaged by exchange rate fluctuations and Brazil's non-tariff protectionist measures. In contrast (and as Figure 4, Figure 10, Figure 12, and Figure 25 show), Brazil is less dependent on Mercosur both in trade and finance, and is determined to maintain a highly regulated process of liberalization because the huge industrial and financial bases inherited from the ISI period are still important, and are the cornerstones of the Brazilian strategy of increased international competitiveness.

---

[125] It is worth noting that after Argentina and Chile, the Uruguayan government also began to publicly express it disappointment with the Brazilian policy toward FTAA. In March 2001 Uruguay's President Jorge Battle announced that if Brazil would refrain from the FTAA negotiations during the 2001 Quebec Third Summit of the Americas, Uruguay was willing to advance unilaterally toward the FTAA "as Chile did". Battle said Uruguay would such as to "recreate the La Plata Viceroyalty" [the Spanish colonial government created in the end of the 18th century] to balance Brazil within Mercosur (La Nación 2001).

Chile is even less dependent than Brazil on Mercosur, and it is better prepared to

negotiate further economic liberalizations, and the persistent differences between its flat

and low tariffs and those of Mercosur (Figure 18) continues to be the most important

impediment to the country's declared interest in full accession to Mercosur[126]. However,

the more Brazil resists further liberalization, the less probable will be the Chilean

accession and Mercosur's expansion because Chile has continued its strategy of trade

diversification[127], and the more intense will be the economic frictions. In fact, since the

---

[126] The average Chilean tariff was 11 percent in 1990, 9% in 2000, scheduled to 6 % by 2003 and to 0 % in 2010. In 2000 Mercosur's CET averaged 14% and. as seen, there had been several unilateral and concerted rises within the Group.

[127] Between 1990 and 1999 Chile signed free trade agreements with Mexico (1991), Venezuela (1993), Colombia and Ecuador (1994), Canada (1997), and Central America (1999). It also signed economic agreements with Argentina (1991), Bolivia (1993), Cuba (1998) and Peru (1998). In 1994 Chile failed to enter the NAFTA Treaty, but succeeded in becoming a full member of the Asia Pacific Economic Cooperation Forum (APEC). In 1996 it signed a political and economic association agreement with the European Union, aimed at a free trade agreement in year 2001 and a political association. In 2000 Chile was negotiating free trade agreements with Bolivia, Japan, South Korea, and the United States, and had received proposals for free trade agreements from India, the European Free Trade Association (EFTA),

1997 Chilean incorporation in the mechanism of Political Consultation and Concertation, in December 2000 Chile and Mercosur experienced their most severe crisis when the Chilean Government--apparently without previous consultation with Mercosur (El Mercurio (2000a)--announced the beginning of bilateral negotiations for a Free Trade Agreement with the United States. In retaliation, the Brazilian Foreign Minister unilaterally announced the suspension of the negotiations for the full Chilean membership in Mercosur (El Mercurio 2000)[128].

However, it could be premature to conclude that the 2000-2001 Mercosur crisis could mean a more general crisis in the Southern Cone process of economic integration, and there are powerful reasons for this. First, none of the countries has advanced a change in its model of development. Therefore, they will all continue their export-led strategies, and for all of them the sub-region continues to be highly attractive, even for Brazil, which cannot discard a sub-regional market that is the base for developing its export-led industrial strategy. This continuity means that economic interdependence will be increased, in turn, makes even more necessary higher levels of economic coordination to prevent further sub-regional imbalances. Second, political concertation will continue to be viable even under more modest forms, if countries perceive more advantages

---

Singapore, Australia, and New Zealand (Ministerio de Relaciones Exteriores 2001c, Rosales 2000).

[128] After the Brazilian reaction the Chilean Foreign Affairs Ministry, Soledad Alvear, insisted that her country "is interested in becoming a full member of Mercosur. But without tariffs parity [with Mercosur], we are going to continue our negotiations with the European Union, the United States and with all those countries interested on" (El Mercurio 2000b). The dispute reached the higher level during the Mercosur's Presidential Summit at Florianapolis, in December 2000, when President Cardoso publicly recriminated the Chilean government, followed by an infuriated President Lagos, who replied: "Do you want to know when are we going to enter the customs union? It does not correspond to us to say, it corresponds to Mercosur to say when are they going to downgrade their tariffs!" (La Nación 2000).

negotiating within Mercosur than without the group, especially regarding the FTAA and the European Union. Third, while trade policy convergence is still uncertain, a structural economic trend toward macroeconomic convergence between the domestic economic processes of the involved countries is observable. As noted before, this process operated unilaterally and de *facto* from 1991 to 2000. However, since then it has become an intergovernmental agreement, and the costs of eventual cheating on the regime have been raised. Fourth, this economic trend toward convergence has been backed by several gestures of political will emanating from the current respective Presidential leaderships, especially those of Brazil and Argentina, and also from Chile.

Therefore, until 2001 the evidence indicated that both the difficulties and the advantages had introduced further incentives for political intergovernmental coordination, in a classic "forward escape", precisely to reduce or avoid the potentially conflictive aspects of increased interdependence and to improve the region's stance at the international level. Further cooperation was agreed at three levels. First, at the sub-regional level, the Mercosur countries agreed to coordinate their macroeconomic policies on the domestic front by adopting a broader perspective in terms of fiscal and monetary policy (negotiations "4+2"). Second, at the inter-regional level, Mercosur continues its negotiations as a block with other economic blocks. Third, at the international level Mercosur, Chile, and Bolivia are coordinating their policies at multilateral institutions, especially regarding their "most effective response to external shocks" (ECLAC 2000:22).

However, many of the positive incentives expected to be seen from increased Mercosur + 2 political cooperation and economic integration remain to be seen, and the basic fact as of April 2001 was that after a decade of increasing economic integration and interdependence, instead of having being strengthened, Mercosur was in critical condition. Because of Brazilian unilateralist behavior, Argentina had abandoned the customs union, which was virtually equal to its disappearance in practical terms, and Chile had been almost expelled and confined to the free trade agreement. The most important conditions for Mercosur's consolidation as a forum for political cooperation, instead of advancing, were experiencing a regression, and several actors (to begin with Cavallo) were even publicly advocating Mercosur's return to the free trade zone.

Therefore, the basic framework upon which rests the eventual development of more advanced types of security cooperation--the second and, especially the third scenario mentioned at the beginning of this chapter--is under stress and indeed seems very improbable not only in the short, but also in the medium term. Neither have Argentina's, Brazil's, and Chile's foreign policies converged enough, particularly in the security realm, nor is Mercosur still on the path toward consolidation as an international economic and political actor.

THIS PAGE INTENTIONALLY LEFT BLANK

# V. CONCLUSIONS. ADVANCES IN AND PROSPECTS FOR SECURITY COOPERATION BETWEEN ARGENTINA, BRAZIL, AND CHILE.

The analysis of Argentine, Brazilian, and Chilean history reveals a clear progress in their inter-state security relationships since 1983 resulting from these states' adoption of a new model of development. After a long first phase featuring the existence of regimes aimed at conflict management, in 1983 the region entered a second phase of building security regimes designed for conflict prevention. Since the mid 1990s, there are germinal manifestations of a third phase moving toward sub-regional collective action in the security field[129]. This evolution has been shaped by three interrelated variables: political democratization, economic liberalization, and sub-regional integration, the causal roles of which have varied along the process.

Chapter II showed that during the first, long phase (1810-1983) rivalry was the outcome of two main successive models of development, featuring hegemonic international rule, oligarchic political regimes, mutual economic isolation and low levels of interdependence, and geopolitical competition for resources, trade, and power. Ideological also factors played a significant role. External ideological devices such as theories of balance of power, geopolitics, and doctrines of total war during the period of the prussianization of the armed forces, and extreme ideologization during the Cold War, were important factors defining perceptions and policies. During this period, however, Argentina, Brazil, and Chile also developed high levels of cooperation prompted by fears of extra-regional hegemonic domination, mutual deterrence, and satisfaction with the

---

[129] We have deliberately avoided the use of the concept of collective security because according to its most extended formulation it has automatic implications of alliance formation.

territorial status quo. However, incentives for cooperation were low and limited, and several periods of crisis arose. Rivalry remained intense, and security cooperation was limited to conflict and crisis management.

The second phase (1983-2001), studied in Chapter III, featured the emergence of democratic regimes, economic liberalization, economic integration, and security cooperation aimed at conflict prevention. The quest for political stability and democratic consolidation, as well as ideological factors by themselves, have been the main causal variables causing the Argentine initiatives that led to new regimes of cooperation with Chile in 1984 and Brazil in 1985. However, while ideological variables have performed as a necessary condition for security cooperation since then, it is unlikely that they would have been sufficient to sustain security cooperation in the long term. In this sense, the adoption of new, neo-liberal economic regimes and strategies of economic integration has been another causal variable, and both have acted to reinforce each other.

During this second period the scope of security cooperation remained essentially sub-regional and, moreover, bilateral, but the sub-region experienced a fundamental strategic change. A contingent democratic peace and economic integration between the three governments from 1990 sparked a change in the countries' intentions and threat perception in relation to one another, minimizing or eliminating traditional conflict hypotheses and raising the demand for more advanced forms of security cooperation to regulate eventual unintended, negative effects of increased economic and societal interdependence. This shift was also reinforced through the institutionalization of more transparent practices regarding policies and strategies. Changes in intentions permitted changes in the capabilities of the states. The most significant shift was the end of the

160

nuclear competition between Argentina and Brazil, but the strategic shift also fostered the adoption of several regimes prohibiting weapons of mass destruction within the region. The development of capabilities also became subject to increased mutual scrutiny, especially through an increasingly dense network of CBMs.

However, changes in conventional military capabilities have been partial, for two main reasons: First, the countries consider territorial defense to be the primary mission of their armed forces even under conditions of increased integration and interdependence, and deterrence continues to be their primary strategic posture. Second, the three countries have developed new types of missions for their armed forces, such as peacekeeping and peace-enforcement, but these are seen as complementary to and not a substitute for territorial defense, and they demand even more sophisticated military capabilities and increased interoperability. Therefore, security cooperation evolved from conflict and crisis management to conflict prevention, but full cooperative security regimes have not been adopted and seem improbable.

The third phase, analyzed in Chapter IV, corresponds to the emergence of sub-regional security regimes within the Southern Cone because of two different but complementary rationales. The first is to address sub-regional transnational security problems that may eventually evolve toward military threats. The second follows from the articulation of Mercosur as a regime of political cooperation able to develop a distinctive common foreign and security policy and to coordinate military action at the international level. However, this third phase is still germinal, and its development is uncertain. It is unclear because Brazilian perceptions of transnational threats are not the same as those of Argentina and Chile, because the countries' foreign policies are divergent on the crucial point of their relationships with the United States, and because the customs union is in crisis. And none of these problems are is likely to be solved in the short or medium run. However, there is still significant room for increased political cooperation and economic integration, and, given the increasing levels of interdependence between these countries, even in the regression scenario, it is reasonable to expect at least the consolidation of the second phase of security cooperation. In sum, the evidence indicates that Southern Cone security cooperation may experience further advances, stagnation, or regression, depending on the evolution of the variables affecting it both vertically (at international, sub-regional, and domestic levels) and horizontally (in the linkages between the economic, political, and security sectors).

This study has thus linked comparative politics and international relations to inform research on integration, by demonstrating the Janus-faced role played by the state in linking levels and sectors. ABC integration has been a processes of regime construction in which states are not the only actors but are still the crucial actors strategically located at the nodal point, articulating private and public actors playing at different levels of analysis and across different sectors. Moreover, states are the only actors in the process acting in a public manner, that is, invested with popular representation to make this articulation of levels and sectors coherent with the interest democratically defined by their polities. Argentine, Brazilian, and Chilean governments have deliberately regulated the pace and nature of integration and security cooperation, subordinating these policies in part to the improvement of their countries' international insertion, but first and foremost to the domestic political stability of their democratic regimes. Therefore, ABC integration must be understood as a strategy deliberately crafted to strengthen and improve Southern Cone states' and societies' capacity for governance, at both domestic and international levels.

Finally, the experience of Southern Cone security cooperation demonstrates that the process has been multi-causal and multilevel, with the role of variables changing over time as the process of integration evolves. Ideology, economic interests, and military power have all acted through different expressions from ABC independence in the early 19th century through the early 21st century. Existing theories of international relations, still mainly realist, liberal, and constructivist schools of thought, continue to study these variables separately instead of integrating them together as different analytical dimensions of a single reality. Nevertheless, and consistently with other studies (Hurrell 1995, Hasenclever *et al* 1997), this thesis points out that explanations for inter-state security cooperation within a context of economic integration and political association, it must be studied using integrated theoretical frameworks, able to articulate multiple variables acting at different levels of analysis and variations in causality during the evolution of the processes.

THIS PAGE INTENTIONALLY LEFT BLANK

# LIST OF REFERENCES

## PRIMARY SOURCES

### Argentina
Balza, Martín, Army Chief of Staff, 1995. "La Seguridad entre los Países del MERCOSUR". *Seguridad Estrategica Regional 8* (October): 25-27.

Ministerio de Defensa Nacional,
----1999a. *Libro Blanco de la Defensa Nacional* (Buenos Aires: Ministerio de Defensa). Available online at [http://www.defensenet.ser2000.org.ar/Archivo/libro-argentina/defa-pI.htm], accessed November 11, 2000.
----1999b. *Libro Blanco de la Defensa Nacional* (Buenos Aires: Ministerio de Defensa). Available online at [http://www.defensenet.ser2000.org.ar/Archivo/libro-argentina/defa-pIV.htm],accessed November 11, 2000.

### Brazil
Cardoso, Fernando Henrique, President of the Federative Republic of Brazil,
----1999. *Progressive Governance for the 21st Century*. Remarks at the Florence Summit, 20-21 November 1999. Available online at [http://www.mre.gov.br/sei/pr-florenca-i.htm], accessed February 7, 2001.
----2000. Speech by President Fernando Henrique Cardoso at the Summit of the Chiefs of State of Mercosul, Bolivia, and Chile, on the Occasion of the XVIII Reunion of the Common Market Counsel. Buenos Aires, June 30. Available at [http://www.mre.gov.br/projeto/mreweb/ingles/discursos/prxviiire-i.htm], accessed February 7, 2001.

Ministério da Defesa, 2001. "Criação do Ministério da defesa era uma idéia antiga". Available online in PDF format at [http://www.defesa.gov.br/historia/historia.htm], accessed May 18, 2001.

Nomar, 2001. "Chega ao Brasil o Nae 'Sao Paulo'". Brazilian Navy official magazine, No. 707, March 5, 2001: 3. Available online at [http://www.mar.mil.br/~gmn/nomar/707_3.htm], accessed May 12, 2001.

Presidência da República, 1996. *Política de Defensa Nacional*. Available online in PDF format at [http://www.defesa.gov.br/politicadedefesa.htm], accessed November 17, 2000.

### Chile
Arancibia Reyes, Jorge P., Admiral, Commandant if Chief, Chilean Navy, 2000. *Conferencia Inaugural Mes del Mar*. May 2000, Chilean Navy Official website, available online at [http://www.armada.cl/armadactual/conferencia00/portada.htm], accessed April 25, 2001.

Couyoumdjian B, Hernán, Vice Admiral, Chief of the National Defense Staff, 1999. *Discurso Aniversario del Estado Mayor de la Defensa Nacional*. Santiago, July 6, 1999.

Fernández B., Mario, Minister of National Defense, 2001. "La Agenda de Defensa". Clase Magistral del Sr. Ministro de Defensa, en la inauguración del ano Académico de las Academias de Guerra y Politécnicas de las FF.AA. Santiago, 14 de marzo de 2001. Available online at the official website of the Chilean Defense Ministry, [http://www.defensa.cl/noti.htm], accessed April 18, 2001.

Insulza, José Miguel, Chilean Foreign Affairs Minister,
----1998a. "Intervención durante el Encuentro Internacional Globalización, América Latina y la II Cumbre de las Américas". In Rojas, A., Francisco (Ed.), *Globalización, América Latina y la Diplomacia de Cumbre* (Santiago: FLACSO-Chile).
----1998b. *Ensayos Sobre Política Exterior* (Santiago: Editorial Los Andes).

Lagos E., Ricardo, Chilean President, 2000. "Discurso de S.E. el Presidente de la República de Chile, D. Ricardo Lagos Escobar, ante el Congreso Pleno de la República Argentina". *Fuerzas Armadas y Sociedad,* Año 15, No. 2, abril-junio.

Ministerio de Defensa Nacional de Chile,
----1997. *Libro de la Defensa Nacional de Chile* (Santiago: Editorial Antártica)
----1999. *Antecedentes de la Cooperación Bilateral en Defensa entre los Gobiernos de Chile y Argentina (1995-1998).* Non-official press working paper. Santiago, April 1999.
----2000. *Ministerio de Defensa Nacional 1994-2000* (Santiago: Ministerio Secretaria General de Gobierno).
----2001.

Ministerio de Relaciones Exteriores de Chile,
----2000a. "Declaración Conjunta". Dirección América del Sur,
[www.minrel.cl/pages/politicos/asur/peru.html], accessed November 17 2000.
----2000b. "República de Argentina". Dirección América del Sur. Available online at [http://www.minrel.cl/pages/politicos/asur/argentina.html], accessed November 17, 2000.
----2000c. "Canciller puntualizó avances en conversaciones con Mercosur". Santiago, October 31. Available online at [http://www.minrel.cl/prensa/Comunicados/31-10-00.htm] accessed April 29, 2001.
----2000d. "Comunicado Conjunto de Argentina, Brazil, Chile y Uruguay Sobre Transporte de Desechos Radiactivos". Santiago, December 22. Available online at [http://www.minrel.cl/prensa/Comunicados/22-12-00/htm}, accessed April 24, 2001.
----2000e. "Se estableció panel de expertos en la OMC para caso del Pez Espada". Santiago, December 12. Available online at
[http://www.minrel.cl/prensa/Comunicados/12-12-00.htm] accessed April 24, 2001.
----2000f. "Ministro formula precisions respecto de negociaciones con Estados Unidos y vinculaciones de Chile con Mercosur". Santiago, December 4. Available online at [http://www.minrel.cl/prensa/Comunicados/04-12-00.htm], accessed April 24, 2001.
----2001a. Dirección América del Sur. Available online at
[http://www.minrel.cl/pages/politicos/asur/index.html], accessed April 4, 2001.
----2001b. "Bolivia". Dirección América del Sur, available online at
[http://www.minrel.cl/pages/politicos/asur/bolivia.html], accessed April 12, 2001.

----2001c. "Acuerdos Económicos Internacionales". Dirección de Relaciones Económicas Internacionales . Available online at [http://www.direcon.cl/acuerdos/index.htm], accessed April 21, 2001.

----2001d. "Mercosur". Dirección América del Sur. Available online at [www.minrel.cl/pages/politicos/asur/mercosur.html], accessed December 9, 2000.

----2001e. "Chile llamó a respetar acuerdo sobre efecto invernadero y a restringir transporte de material radioactivo". Santiago, April 25, 2001. Available online at [http://www.minrel.cl/prensa/Comunicados/2001/25-04-01.htm], accessed May 4, 2001.

Pérez Yoma, Edmundo, Chilean Minister of National Defense,

----1997. *Los Desafíos de la Seguridad y Defensa en el Cono Sur*. Red de Información ESIP-SER en el 2000. Database "Defensa y Confianza Mutua en el Cono Sur". Available online at [http://www.defensenet.ser2000.org.ar/Archivo/d000d320.htm], accessed February 8, 2001.

----1999. "La Defensa Nacional de Chile y la Globalización". *Fuerzas Armadas y Sociedad*, Año 14, No. 4, Octubre-Diciembre. Available online at [http://www.flacso.cl/index.htm], accessed April 18, 2001.

Valdés, Juan Gabriel, 1999, Chilean Foreign Minister. "Diez Años de APEC: Proyecciones Diplomáticas y Comerciales". Remarks at the Chilean-New Zealand Chamber of Commerce, September 4.

**United States of America**

Central Intelligence Agency (CIA) 2001. *CIA World Factbook*. Available online at [http://www.odci.gov/cia/publications/factbook/index.html], accessed May 31, 2001.

Marrero, Victor, U.S. Permanent Representative to the Organization of American States, 1999. *Remarks to the OAS Permanent Council*. Washington, D.C., May 12. Available online at [http://www.state.gov/www/policy_remarks/1999/990512_marrero_oas.html], accessed April 29, 2001.

United States State Department,

----2000. "Chile Declassification Project: Final Release". Statement by Richard Boucher, Spokesman, November 13, 2000, Media Note. United States State Department, Office of the Spokesman, Press Statement. Available Online at [http://secretary.state.gov/www/briefings/statements/2000/ps001113b.html], accessed April 2, 2001.

----2001. "Background Note: Ecuador". Bureau of Western Hemisphere Affairs April 2001. Available online at [http://www.state.gov/r/pa/bgn/index.cfm?docid=2020], accessed April 18, 2001.

United States Department of Commerce, 2000. "Chile". International Trade Administration, Market Access and Compliance. Available online at [http://www.mac.doc.gov/ola/mercosur/factsheet%20-%20chile.htm], accessed July 17, 2000.

United States Southern Command, 2000. U.S. Special Operation Forces participate in multinational Peacekeeping exercise". Miami, August 18. Available online at [http://www.southcom.mil/pa/news/news000818a.htm], accessed May 3, 2001.

**International institutions**
Common Market of the South (Mercosur),
----1997. "Comunicado Conjunto de los Presidentes de los Estados Partes. Comunicado del 19 de junio de 1997, Asunción". Mercosur Secretariat, Montevideo, Official website, available online at [http://www.mercosur.org.uy], accessed April 30, 2001.
----2001. "Comunicados Conjuntos de los Presidentes
en Reuniones Cumbre del MERCOSUR". Mercosur Secretariat, Montevideo, Official website, available online at [http://www.mercosur.org.uy], accessed April 30, 2001.

General Agreement of Trade and Tariffs (GATT), 1992. *International Trade 90-91. Volume II* (Geneva: GATT).

Inter American Development Bank (IADB),
----1999. "Integration and Trade in the Americas". Periodic Note on Integration and Trade in the America, October. Available online in PDF format at [http://www.iadb.org/int/itd/english/periodic_notes/note1099.pdf], accessed April 9, 2001.
----199a. "Integration and Trade in the Americas. Special Report. The International Financial Crisis: Implications for Latin American and Caribbean Trade and Integration". Periodic Note on Integration and Trade in the America, October. Available online in PDF format at [http://www.iadb.org/int/itd/english/periodic_notes/note1099.pdf], accessed April 9, 2001.

----2000. "Integration and Trade in the Americas". Periodic Note on Integration and Trade in the America". December . Available online in PDF format at [http://www.iadb.org/int/itd/english/periodic_notes/np1200eng.pdf], accessed April 9, 2001.

International Monetary Fund (IMF),
----2001. "Argentina: Second Review Under the Stand-By Arrangement and Request for Augmentation. Staff Report; Staff Statement; Press Release on the Executive Board Discussion. Country Report No. 01/26". Washington D.C., January 26. Available online in PDF format at [http://www.imf.org/external/pubs/cat/longres.cfm?sk&sk=3903.0], accessed April 24, 2001.
----2001a. Brazil: Selected Issues and Statistical Appendix. Country Report No. 01/10". Washington D.C., January 11. Available online in PDF format at [http://www.imf.org/external/pubs/cat/longres.cfm?sk&sk=3884.0], accessed April 24, 2001.
----2001b. Chile: Selected Issues. IMF Staff Country Report No. 00/104. Washington D.C., August 23. Available online in PDF format at [http://www.imf.org/external/pubs/cat/longres.cfm?sk&sk=3662.0], accessed April 24, 2001.

Organization of American States (OAS),

----2001a. Conventions and Treaties. Available online at [http://www.oas.org/], accessed April 8, 2001.

----2001b. Inventory of Confidence- and Security -Building Measures applied by the Member States of the OAS 1996 -1999. Document prepared by the General Secretariat. Available online at [http://www.oas.org/], accessed April 8, 2001.

Summit of the Americas Information Network (SAIN),

----1998. Second Summit of the Americas. *Declaración de Santiago*. Available online at [http://www.summit-americas.org/Hemispheric%20Security/Santiago-Security-eng.htm], accessed March 2000.

----2001. "Declaration of Quebec City". Quebec City, Canada, April 20-22, 2001. available online at [http://www.summit-americas.org/Documents%20for%20Quebec%20City%20Summit/Quebec/Declaration%20of%20Quebec%20City%20-%20Eng%20-%20final.htm]

United Nations Economic Commission for Latin America and the Caribbean (ECLAC),

----2000. *Preliminary Overview of the Economies of Latin America and the Caribbean 2000* (Santiago: ECLAC). Also available online in PDF format at [http://www.eclac.cl/cgi-bin/getProd.asp?xml=/publicaciones/xml/1/5841/P5841.xml&xsl=/tpl-i/p9f.xsl&base=\tpl-i\top-bottom.xsl], accessed April 24, 2001.

----2000a. *Estudio Económico de América latina y el Caribe 1999-2000* (Santiago: ECLAC). Available online in PDF format at [http://www.eclac.cl/cgi-bin/getProd.asp?xml=/publicaciones/xml/9/4919/P4919.xml&xsl=/tpl/p9f.xsl], accessed April 23, 2001.

United Nations Institute for Disarmament Research (UNIDIR, 1990. *Nonoffensive Defense. A Global perspective* (New York: Taylor & Francis).

World Bank, 2000. *Entering the 21$^{st}$ Century. World Development Report 1999/2000*. Available online in PDF format at [http://www.worldbank.org/wdr/2000/fullreport.html], accessed March 17, 2001.

## SECONDARY SOURCES

### Newspapers

Clarín (Argentina), 2001. "Cavallo les pidió a los brasileños que confíen en la convertibilidad" Buenos Aires, April 19. Available online at [http://ar.clarin.com/diario/2001-04-19/e-00601.htm], accessed April 27, 2001.

El Mercurio (Chile).
----2000. "Mercosur suspende negociaciones con Chile". Santiago, December 4. Available online at

[http://www.emol.com/noticias/detalle/detalle_noticia.asp?idnoticia=40107], accessed April 12, 2000.

----2000a. "Revuelo en el vecindario. Efectos del Acuerdo Chile-EE.UU.". Santiago, December 10. Available online at [http://www.emol.com/diario-elmercurio/reportajes_v/705801901011012200005J0160059.asj], accessed December 10, 2000.

----2000b. "Se Complica Ingreso Chileno a Mercosur por TLC con EE.UU.". Santiago, December 5. Available online at [http://www.emol.com/noticias/detalle/detalle_diario.asp?idnoticia=0105122000001A00 10168], accessed December 5, 2000.

----2000c. "Chile en el Mercosur Entra en 'Periodo de Reflexión'". Santiago, December 9. Available online at [http://www.emol.com/noticias/detalle/detalle_diario.asp?idnoticia=0109122000001A00 10020], accessed December 9, 2000.

----2000d. "Mercosur y Chile Fijan Metas Económicas". Available online at [[http://www.mre.gov.br/acs/interclip/jornais/dezembro/mercurio15a.htm]. Accessed April 22, 2001.

----2001. "Arancel Efectivo Cae a Mínimo Histórico: 5,9%". Santiago, March 20. Available online at [http://www.emol.com/diario_elmercurio/eyn], accessed March 21, 2001

----2001a. "Los 10 anos de Mercosur: ¿Y que Cumplas Muchos Más?". Santiago, April 1. Available online at [http://www.emol.com/diario_elmercurio/eyn], accessed April 1, 2001.


Financial Times, 2001. "Cavallo mulls Mercosur break". London, April 18. Available online at [http://globalarchive.ft.com/globalarchive/articles.html?id=010418011782&query=Cavall o+mulls+Mercosur+break], accessed May 9, 2001.


La Nación (Argentina),
----2000. "De la Rúa medió entre Lagos y Cardoso". Buenos Aires, December 16. Available online at [http://www.mre.gov.br/acs/interclip/jornais/dezembro/nacion18a.htm], accessed April 22, 2001.

----2001. "Nuevas dudas sobre el futuro del Mercosur". Buenos Aires, March 18, 2001. Available online at [http://www.mre.gov.br/acs/interclip/jornais/marco01/nacion19b.htm], accessed April 22, 2001.

----2001a. "Defense apuesta a fortalecer la unión del Mercosur". Buenos Aires, April 10, 2001. Available online at [http://www.mre.gov.br/acs/interclip/jornais/abril01/nacion10c.html], accessed April 27, 2001.


The New York Times,
----2001. "Official Sees Stability for Argentina in Currency Move". New York, April 17, 2001. Available online at

[http://www.nytimes.com/2001/04/17/business/17ARGE.html?searchpv=site07], accessed April 24, 2001.

----2001a. "Argentina May Peg Peso to Euro as Well as Dollar". New York, April 12. Available on-line at [http://www.nytimes.com/2001/04/12/business/12ARGE.html?searchpv=site12], accessed April 24, 2001.


**Magazines**

América Economía,

----2000. "Bye Bye, Mercosur". Published December 28. Available online at [http://www.americaeconomia.com/Content_Articles.asp?ID=15793], accessed March 26, 2001.

----2000a. "Comercio: Unión Sin Rumbo". Published May 18. Available online at [http://www.americaeconomia.com/Content_Articles.asp?ID=10343], accessed March 26, 2001.


Flight International 2001. London, May 1-7, 2001.


The Economist, 2001. "Another Blow to Mercosur", March 31: 17, 33-4.


**Other electronic media**

Stratfor.com, 1999. "U.S. proposes Intervention forces for Latin American Crises". Colombia. Global Intelligence Update, June 10. Available online at [http://www.stratfor.com/SERVICES/GIU/061099.ASP], accessed September 28, 2000.


**Books and scholarly papers**

Abad Cid, Hernán, 1994 (2000). "Catastro Nacional de Fronteras Interiores de Chile". Reprinted in Meirelles, Carlos, *Antología Geopolítica de Autores Militares Chilenos* (Santiago: Centro de Estudios e Investigaciones Militares).


Acharya, Amitav, 1998. "Collective Identity and Conflict Management in South East Asia". In Adler, Emanuel, and Barnett, Michael (Eds.), *Security Communities* (Cambridge: Cambridge University Press).


Adler, Emanuel, and Barnett, Michael,

----1998a. "Security Communities in theoretical perspective". In Adler, Emanuel, and Barnett, Michael (Eds.), *Security Communities* (Cambridge: Cambridge University Press).

----1998b. "A framework for the study of security communities". In Adler, Emanuel, and Barnett, Michael (Eds.), *Security Communities* (Cambridge: Cambridge University Press).


Aggarwal, Vinod K, 1985. *Liberal Protectionism. The International Politics of Organized Textile Trade* (Berkeley: University of California Press).


Agüero, Felipe,

171

----1995. *Soldiers, Civilians, and Democracy. Post-Franco Spain in Comparative Perspective* (Baltimore: The Johns Hopkins University Press).
----2000. "Transition Pathways: Institutional Legacies, the Military, and Democracy". In Hollifield, James F., and Jillson, Calvin (Eds.), *Pathways to Democracy: The Political Economy of Democratic Transitions* (New York: Routledge).

Alagappa, Muthiah,
----1998a. "International Politics in Asia. The Historical context". In Alagappa, Muthiah, *Asian Security Practice. Material and ideational Influences* (Stanford: Stanford University Press).
----1998b. "Asian Practices of Security. Key features and Explanations". In Alagappa, Muthiah, *Asian Security Practice. Material and ideational Influences* (Stanford: Stanford University Press).
----1998c. "Conceptualizing Security. Hierarchy and Conceptual Traveling". In Alagappa, Muthiah, *Asian Security Practice. Material and ideational Influences* (Stanford: Stanford University Press).
Anderson, Jeffrey (Ed.), 1999. *European Integration and Democracy. Expanding on the European Experience* (Lanham: Rowman and Littlefield).

Allison, Graham, and Zelikow, Philip, 1999. *The Essence of decision. Explaining the Cuban Missile Crisis. Second Edition* (New York: Longman).

Atkins, Pope, 1977 (1995). *Latin America in the International Political System. Third Edition* (Boulder, CO.: Westview Press).

Atria, Rodrigo, 2000. "Estado, Militares y Democracia: La afirmación de la supremacía civil en Chile" *Fuerzas Armadas y Sociedad*, Año 15, No. 1, enero-marzo.

Avendaño R., Andrés, Col. Chilean Army, 1997. "Entre la Cooperación y el Conflicto". *Revista Memorial del Ejército de Chile*, No. 453.

Averbug, Marcello, 2000. "Argentina". IADB Country Report 2000. Available online at [http://www.iadb.org/int/sta/ENGLISH/staweb/#regrpt], accessed April 23, 2001.

Bagby, Wesley M., 1999. *America's International Relations Since World, War I* (New York: Oxford University Press).

Baer, Werner, and Paiva, Claudio, 1997. "Brazil". In Randall, Laura (Ed.), *The Political Economy of Latin America in the Postwar Period* (Austin: University of Texas Press).

Balassa, Bela, 1961. *The Theory of Economic Integration* (Homewood: Richard D. Irwin).

Barletta, Michael,
----1999. "Democratic Security and Diversionary Peace: Nuclear Confidence-Building in Argentina and Brazil". *National Security Studies Quarterly*, Summer: 19-38.

172

----2000. *Ambiguity, Autonomy, and the Atom: Emergence of the Argentine-Brazilian Nuclear Regime*. Ph.D. dissertation. Department of Political Science, University of Wisconsin-Madison.

Bergsten, C. Fred, 1997. "Open Regionalism". *The World Economy*, Vol. 20, august 5: 545-565.

Borón, Atilio, 1998. "Faulty Democracies? A Reflection on the Capitalist 'Fault Lines'". In Agüero, Felipe and Stark, Jeffrey (Eds.), *Fault Lines of Democracy in Post-Transition Latin America* (Boulder, CO.: Lynne Rienner Publishers).

Buchanan, Paul G., 1998. "Chameleon, Tortoise, or Toad. The Changing U.S. Security Policy in Contemporary Latin America". In Domínguez, Jorge (Ed.), *International Security and Democracy. Latin America and the Caribbean in the Post-Cold War Era* (Pittsburgh: University of Pittsburgh Press).

Budnevich, Carlos, and Zahler, Roberto, 1999. *Integración Financiera y Coordinación Macroeconómica en el Mercosur*. Central Bank of Chile, Working Papers No. 52, December. Available online in PDF format at [www.bcentral.cl/Estudios/DTBC/doctrab.htm], accessed February 10, 2001, 39 pp.

Burr, Robert , 1967. *By Reason or Force. Force. Chile and the Balancing of Power in South America, 1830-1905* (Berkeley: University of California Press).

Burns, E. Bradford, 1994. *Latin America. A Concise Interpretative History. Sixth Edition* (Englewood Cliffs, N.J.: Prentice Hall).

Buzan, Barry, Weaver, Ole, and De Wilde, Jaap, 1998. *Security. A New Framework for Analysis* (Boulder: Lynne Rienner Publisher).

Cáceres, Gustavo, and Scheetz, Thomas (Eds.), 1995. *Defensa No Provocativa* (Buenos Aires: Editora Buenos Sires).

Cañas M., Ramón, 1956 (2000). "Chile en el Pacífico, Argentina en el Atlántico, Factores de Estabilidad Continental". Reprinted in Meirelles, Carlos, *Antología Geopolítica de Autores Militares Chilenos* (Santiago: Centro de Estudios e Investigaciones Militares).

Cardoso, Eliana, and Helwege, Ann, 1992 (1999). *Latin America's economy: Diversity, Trends, and Conflicts* (Cambridge: The MIT Press).

Caro, Isaac, 1994. "Cooperación Pacífica y Medidas de Confianza Mutua en Chile". In Varas, Augusto, and Caro, Isaac, *Medidas de Confianza Mutua en América Latina* (Santiago: FLACSO-Chile/Stimson Center/SER).

Carter, Ashton B.; Perry, William J.; and Steinbruner, John D., 1992 (1997). "A New Concept of Cooperative Security". *Strategy and Force Planning. Second Edition* (Newport R.I.: Naval War College Press).

Castro, Jorge, 1998. "Perspectivas estratégicas de Argentina a fin de siglo". In Diamint, Rut (Ed.), *Argentina y la Seguridad Internacional* (Santiago: FLACSO-Chile/W. Wilson Center/Colección Paz y Seguridad en las Américas).

Cavallo, Domingo, 2001. *Pasión Por Crear* (Buenos Aires: Planeta).

Cheyre, Emilio, 2000. *Medidas de Confianza Mutua: Casos de América Latina y el Mediterráneo* (Santiago: Centro de Estudios e Investigaciones Militares).

Child, Jack, 1990. "The Status of South American Geopolitical Thinking". In Atkins, Pope (Ed.), *South America into the 1990s: Evolving Relationships in a New Era* (Boulder, CO.: Westview Press).

Clausewitz, Carl Von, 1993. *On War. Edited and translated by Michael Howard and Peter Paret* (New York: Alfred Knopf).

Cope, John A., 1998. "Hemispheric Security Relations. Remodeling the U.S. Framework for the Americas". Strategic Forum, Institute for National Strategic Studies, National Defense University, Number 147, September. Available online at [http://www.ndu.edu/inss/strforum/forum147.html], accessed March 2000.

Corrales, Javier, and Feinberg, Richard E., 1999. "Regimes of Cooperation in the Western Hemisphere: Power, Interests, and Intellectual Traditions". *International Studies Quarterly*, Vol. 43, No. 1: 1-36.

Costa Vaz, Alcides, 1999. "La Politica Exterior brasilena: Prioridades Estratégicas, Alianzas e Implicaciones para el MERCOSUR. In Rojas A., Francisco (Ed.). *Argentina, Brasil y Chile: Integragion y Seguridad* (Santiago: FLACSO-Chile/Nueva Sociedad, 1999).

Cottan, Martha L., 1994. *Images & Intervention. U.S. Policies in Latin America* (Pittsburgh: University of Pittsburgh Press).

Cruz, Consuelo, and Diamint, Rut, 1998. "The New Military Autonomy in Latin America". *Journal of Democracy*, Vol. 9, No. 4: 115-127.

Diamond, Larry, 1996. "Democracy in Latin America. Degrees, Illusions, and Directions or Consolidation". In Farer, Tom (Ed.), *Beyond Sovereignty. Collectively Defending Democracy in the Americas* (Baltimore: The Johns Hopkins University Press).

Diamond, Larry; Hartlyn, Jonathan; Linz, Juan J.; and Lipset, Seymour Martin (Eds.), 1999. *Democracy in Developing Countries. Latin America. Second Edition* (Boulder: Lynne Rienner Publishers).

Disnmoor, James, 200. "Brazil". IADB Country Report 2000. Available online at [http://www.iadb.org/int/sta/ENGLISH/staweb/#regrpt], accessed April 23, 2001.

Deutsch, Karl et. al., 1957. *Political Community and the North Atlantic Area* (Princeton, N.J.: Princeton University Press).

Devlin, Robert, Estevadeordal, Antoni, and Garay, Jorge Luis, 1999. "The FTAA: Some Longer Term Issues". Intal/ITD. Occasional Paper 5, August.

Donnelly, Jack, 1991. "Progress in human Rights". In Adler, Emanuel, and Crawford, Beverly (Eds.), *Progress in Postwar International Relations* (New York: Columbia University Press).

Dougherty, James E., and Pfaltzgraff, Robert L. Jr., 1997. *Contending Theories on International Relations. A comprehensive Survey. Fourth Edition* (New York: Longman).

Doyle, Michael W.,
----1983. "Kant, Liberal Legacies, and Foreign Affairs". In *Philosophy and Public Affairs*, Vol. 12, Nos. 3-4 (Summer and Fall, 1983): 205-35, 323-53.
----1986. "Liberalism and World Politics". *American Political Science Review*, Vol. 80: 1161.
----1997. *Ways of War and Peace* (New York: W.W. Norton and Company).

Economic Commission for Latin America and the Caribbean (ECLAC),
----1994. *Open Regionalism in Latin America and the Caribbean* (Santiago: ECLAC).
----1999. "The New Multilateral Trade Negotiations: A Challenge for Latin America and the Caribbean", paper prepared by ECLAC for the Third Ministerial Conference of the World Trade Organization (WTO), Seattle, 30 November-3 December.

Ensalaco, Mark, 1995. "Military Prerogatives and the Stalemate of Chilean Civil-Military Relations". *Armed Forces and Society*, Vol. 21, No. 2: 255-70.

Escudé, Carlos,
----1991. *Realismo Periférico. Fundamentos para la Nueva Política ExteriorArgentina* (Buenos Aires: Planeta).
----1998. "An Introduction to Peripheral Realism and Its Implications for the Interstate System: Argentina and the Condor II Missile Project". In Neumann, Stephanie G. (Ed.), *International Relations Theory and the Third World* (New York: St. Martin's Press).
----1999. "Argentina y sus Alianzas Estratégicas". In Rojas A., Francisco (Ed.), *Argentina, Brasil y Chile: Integracion y Seguridad* (Santiago: FLACSO-Chile/Nueva Sociedad).

Escudé, Carlos and Fontana, Andrés, 1998. "Argentina's Security Policies. Their Rationale and Regional Context". In Domínguez, Jorge (Ed.), *International Security and Democracy. Latin America and the Caribbean in the Post-Cold War Era* (Pittsburgh: University of Pittsburgh Press).

Etzioni, Amitai, 1965. *Political Unification: A Comparative Study of leaders and Forces* (New York: Holt, Rinehart and Winston).

Farer, Tom, 1996. "Collectively Defending Democracy in the Western Hemisphere. Introduction and Overview". In Farer, Tom (Ed.), *Beyond Sovereignty. Collectively Defending Democracy in the Americas* (Baltimore: The Johns Hopkins University Press).

Fawcett, Louise and Hurrell, Andrew (Eds.), 1995. *Regionalism in World Politics. Regional Organization and International Order* (New York: Oxford University Press).

Fernández B., Mario, 1997. "El Sistema Político Chileno: Características y tendencias". In Toloza, Cristián, and Lahera, Eugenio, *Chile en los Noventa* (Santiago: Presidencia de la República/Dolmen Ediciones).

Fernández de Castro, Rafael, and Rosales, Carlos A., 2000. "Migration Issues: Rising the Stakes in U.S. Latin American Relations". In Domínguez, Jorge I. (Ed.), *The Future of Inter-American Relations* (New York: Routledge).

Fitch, Samuel J., 1994. "The Decline of U.S. Military Influence in Latin America". In Schoultz, Lars; Smith, Williams; and Varas, Augusto F., *Security, Democracy and Development in the Western Hemisphere* (Miami: North-South Center Press, University of Miami).

Fournier, Dominique, 1999. "The Alfonsín Administration and the Promotion of the Democratic Values in the Southern Cone and the Andes". *Journal of Latin American Studies*, Vol. 31, Part I, February: 39-74.

Franko, Patrice M., 2000. *Toward a New security Architecture in the Americas. Strategic Implications of the FTAA* (Washington D.C.: The CSIS Press).

Freedman, Lawrence, 1998. "The Revolution in Strategic Affairs". *Adelphi Paper 318* (Oxford: Oxford University Press).

Frieden, Jeffrey, Pastor, Manuel Jr., and Tomz, Michael E. (Eds.), 2000. *Modern Political Economy and Latin America. Theory and Policy* (Boulder: Westview Press).

Frohman, Alicia, 1990. *Puentes Sobre la Turbulencia. La Concertacion Politica Latinoamericana en los Ochenta* (Santiago: FLACSO-Chile).

Fuentes, Claudio,

----1997. "Interdependencia y Seguridad". *Fuerzas Armadas y Sociedad,* Año 12, No. 1, enero-Marzo: 3-36.

----2000. *Elite Cleavages and Military Subordination in Chile.* Paper presented on the XXII International Congress of the Latin American Studies Association, LASA, Miami, March 16-18, 2000.

García C., Jaime, 1985 (2000). "Reflexiones Sobre el Núcleo Vital de Chile". Reprinted in Meirelles, Carlos, *Antología Geopolítica de Autores Militares Chilenos* (Santiago: Centro de Estudios e Investigaciones Militares).

García, Gonzalo, and Montes, Juan Esteban, 1994. *Subordinación Democrática de los Militares. Exitos y Fracasos en Chile* (Santiago: CED).

Garretón, Manuel Antonio, 1989. *The Chilean Political Process* (Boston: Unwin Hyman).

Gartzke, Erik; Li, Quan; and Boehmer, Charles, 2001. "Investing in the Peace: Economic Interdependence and International Conflict". *International Organization*, Vol. 55, No. 2, Spring: 391-438.

Gaspar, Gabriel, 1999. "La Política de Defensa de Chile". In Rojas A., Francisco (Ed.), *Argentina, Brasil y Chile: Integracion y Seguridad* (Santiago: FLACSO-Chile/Nueva Sociedad).

Gazmuri, Jaime, 1997. "Rol del Congreso, Fuerzas Armadas y Estado Democrático". *Fuerzas Armadas y Sociedad*, Año 12, No. 4, Octubre-Diciembre 1997, FLACSO-Chile, Santiago.

Gillis, Malcolm; Perkins, Dwight H.; Roemer, Michael; and Snodgrass, Donald R., 1996. *Economics of Developing Countries. Fourth Edition* (New York: W.W. Norton & Company).

Gilpin, Robert, 1987. *The Political Economy of International Relations* (Princeton: Princeton University Press).

Glaser, Charles 1995. "Realist as Optimists. Cooperation as Self-Help". In Brown, Michael; Cote Jr., Owen; Lynn-Jones, Sean M.; and Miller, Steven E., *Theories of War and Peace. An International Security Reader* (Cambridge, Mass.: The MIT Press).

Glennon, Michael, 1999. "The New Interventionism", Foreign Affairs, May/June 1999.

Grieco, Joseph M., 1988. "Anarchy and the limits of cooperation: A realist critique of the newest liberal institutionalism". *International Organization* 42, 3, Summer: 485-507.

Guedes da Costa, Thomas,
----1998. "Strategic Balance, Brazil, and Western Hemispheric Security". In Tulchin, Joseph S., Rojas Aravena, Francisco, and Espach, Ralph H., (Eds.), *Strategic Balance*

*and Confidence Building Measures in the Americas* (Washington, D.C./Stanford, CA: The Woodrow Wilson Center Press/Stanford University Press).
---- 2000. *Brazil in the New Decade. Searching for a Future* (Washington D.C.: Center for Strategic and International Studies).

Guilhon Alburquerque, José Augusto, 1999. "Mercosur: Democratic Stability and Economic Integration in South America". In Anderson, Jeffrey (Ed.), *European Integration and Democracy. Expanding on the European Experience* (Lanham: Rowman and Littlefield).

Haas, Ernst B.,
----*The Uniting of Europe: Political, Social, and Economic Forces, 1950-1957* (Stanford: Stanford University Press).
----1966. "International Integration: The European and the Universal Process". In *International Political Communities: An Anthology* (New York: Doubleday).
----1968. *The Uniting of Europe: Social, Political, and Economic Forces, 1950-57* (Stanford: Stanford University Press).

Haggard, Stephan, and Kaufman, Robert R., 1995. *The Political Economy of Democratic Transitions* (Princeton: Princeton University Press).

Hasenclever, Andreas; Mayer, Peter; and Rittberger, Volker, 1996. "Interests', Power, and Knowledge: The Study of International Regimes". *Mershon International Studies Review,* Vol. 40, Supplement 2, October: 177-228.

Hirst, Monica,
----1996. "The Foreign Policy of Brazil: From the Democratic Transition to Its Consolidation". In Muñoz, Heraldo, and Tulchin, Joseph S. (Eds.), *Latin American Notions in World Politics. Second Edition* (Boulder: Westview Press).
----1998. "Politicas de Seguridad, Democratizacion e Integracion Regional en el Cono Sur". In Jorge Domínguez (Ed.), *Seguridad Internacional, Paz y Democracia en el Cono Sur* (Santiago: FLASCO-Chile/Dialogo Interamericano).
----1999. "Mercosur's Complex Political Agenda". In Roett, Riordan (Ed.), *MERCOSUR. Regional Integration, World Markets* (Boulder, CO.: Lynne Rienner Publishers).

Holsti, K. J., 1992. "International Theory and War in the Third World". In Job, Brian L., (Ed.), *The Insecurity Dilemma. National Security of the Third World States* (Boulder: Lynne Rienner Publishers).

Holz, Eva, 1999. "The 'Samba' Effect in Mercosur". *SELA Publications. Latin America in the International Financial Crisis.* Edition No. 56, May-August, available at [www.lanic.itexas.edu/project/sela/eng_capitulos/rcapin56-6.htm], accessed February 29 2000.

Hoffmann, Stanley

----1966. "Obstinate or Obsolete: the Fate of the Nation-State and the Case of the Western Europe". *Daedelus*, Vol. 95: 862-915.
----1982. "Reflections on the Nation-State in Western Europe Today". *Journal of Common Market Studies*, Vol. 21: 21-37.

Hunter, Wendy,
----1996. *State, Soldier in Latin America. Redefining the Military's Role in Argentina, Brazil, and Chile* (Washington D.C.:. Unites States Institute of Peace Press).
----1997. Eroding Military Influence in Brazil. Politicians Against Soldiers (Chapel Hill: University of North Carolina Press).

Huntington, Samuel, 1991. *The Third Wave. Democratization in the Late Twentieth Century* (Norman: University of Oklahoma Press).

Hurrel, Andrew,
----1995. "Regionalism in Theoretical perspective". In Fawcet,, Louise, and Hurrell, Andrew (Eds.), *Regionalism in World Politics. Regional Organization and International Order* (Oxford: Oxford University Press).
----1998a. "An emerging security community in South America?". In Adler, Emmanuel, and Barnett, Michael, *Security Communities* (Cambridge: Cambridge University Press).
----1998b. "Security in Latin America". *International Affairs*, Vol. 74, No. 3: 529-46.

Independent Commission for Disarmament and Security Issues, 1982. *Common Security. A Blueprint for Survival* (New York: Simon and Schuster).

International Institute for Strategic Studies (IISS),
----1991. *The Military Balance 1990-199* (London: Brassey's).
----2001. *The Military Balance 2000-2001* (Oxford: Oxford University Press).

Jaguaribe, 1998. "MERCOSUR y las Alternativas del Orden Mundial". In Rojas A., Francico (Ed.), *Globalizacion, América Latina y Diplomacia de Cumbres* (Santiago: FLACSO-Chile).

Jervis, Robert,
----1978. "Cooperation Under Security Dilemma". World Politics 30 (January): 167-214.
----1999. "Realism Liberalism, and Cooperation. Understanding the Debate".
*International Security*, Vol. 24, No.1 (Summer): 42-63.

Jones, Rodney; McDonough, Mark G; Dalton, Toby F.; and Koblentz, Gregory D., 1998. *Tracking Nuclear Proliferation. A Guide in Maps and Charts, 1998* (Washington, D.C: The Carnegie Endowment for International Peace).

Kacowicz, 1998. *Zones of Peace in the Third World. South America and West Africa in Comparative Perspective* (New York: State University of New York Press).

Kennedy, Paul,

----1976 (1998). *The Rise and Fall of British Naval Mastery. Third Edition* (New York: Humanity Books).

---- (Ed.), 1991. *Grand Strategies in War and Peace* (New Haven: Yale University Press).

Keohane, 1984. *After Hegemony: Cooperation and Discord in the World Political Economy (Princeton: Princeton University Press).*

Keohane, Robert O., and Hoffman, Stanley, 1991. *The New European Community. Decisionmaking and Institutional Change* (Boulder: Westview Press).

Keohane, Robert O. and Martin, Lisa L., 1995. *The Promise of Institutionalist Theory.* Reprinted in Michael E. Brown, Owen R. Coté Jr., Sean M. Lynn-Jones and Steven E. Miller, *Theories of War and Peace. An International Security Reader* (Cambridge: The MIR Press, 2000).

Keohane, Robert O. and Nye, Joseph S. Jr., 1977 (2001). *Power and Interdependence. Third Edition* (New York: Longman).

Keylor, William R.,1996. *The Twentieth Century World. An International History*( New York: Oxford University Press).

Klarén, Peter F., 1986. "Lost Promise: Explaining Latin American Underdevelopment". In Klarén, Peter, and Bossert, Thomas J., *Promise of Development. Theories of Change in Latin America* (Boulder: Westview Press).

Krasner, Stephen
----1982. "Structural Causes and Regime Consequences: regimes as Intervening Variables". *International Organization*, Vol. 36, No. 2, Spring: 185-205.
----- (Ed.), 1983. *International Regimes* (Ithaca, N.Y.: Cornell University Press).

Krepinovich, Andrew F., 1994. "Cavalry to Computer. The Pattern of Military Revolutions". *The National Interest*, Fall: 30-42).

Krepon, Michael, and Varas, Augusto, 1994. "Prefacio". In Varas, Augusto, and Caro, Isaac, *Medidas de Confianza Mutua en América Latina* (Santiago: FLACSO-Chile/Stimson Center/SER).

Kupchan, Charles A., and Kupchan, Clifford A., 1995. "The Promise of Collective Security". *International Security* Vol. 20, No. 1 (Summer): 52-61.

Lagorio, Ricardo E., 1998. "Institutionalization, Cooperative Security, and peacekeeping Operations. The Argentine Experience". In Domínguez, Jorge (Ed.), *International Security and Democracy. Latin America and the Caribbean in the Post-Cold War Era* (Pittsburgh: University of Pittsburgh Press).

Lamounier, Bolívar, 1999. "Brazil. Inequality Against Democracy". In Diamond, Larry; Hartlyn, Jonathan; Linz, Juan J.; and Lipset, Seymour Martin (Eds.). *Democracy in Developing Countries. Latin America. Second Edition* (Boulder, CO.: Lynne Rienner Publishers).

Layne, Christopher,
----1993 (1997). "The Unipolar Illusion. Why New Great Powers Will Rise". Reprinted in Lynn-Jones, Sean M., and Miller, Steen E. (Eds.), *The Cold War and After. Prospects for Peace. Expanded Edition* (Cambridge: The MIT Press, 2000).
----1994 (2000). "Kant or Cant. The Myth of the Democratic Peace". Reprinted in Brown, Michael E.; Coté Jr., Owen R.; Lynn-Jones, Sean M.; and Miller, Steven E., *Theories of War and Peace. An International Security Reader* (Cambridge: The MIT Press, 2000).

Lechini, Gladys, 1998. "Concertación regional en América Latina. Opciones radicionales y nuevas alternatives". In Rojas A., Francisco (Ed.), *Globalización, América Latina y la Diplomacia de Cumbre* (Santiago: FLACSO-Chile).

LeFort V., Guillermo, 2000. *Los Resultados Macroeconómicos del gobierno de Eduardo Frei Ruiz-Tagle: Una Evaluación Comparativa*. Central Bank of Chile, Working Papers No. 81, October.

Leite Ribeiro, Guilherme, 1997. "La Consolidación del Mercosur como proceso integrador". In Milet, Paz; Gaspar, Gabriel; and Rojas A., Francisco (Eds.), *Chile-MERCOSUR: Una alianza Estratégica* (Santiago: FLASO-Chile).

LeRoy Bennett, A, 1995. *International Organizations* (Englewood Cliffs, N.J.: Prentice Hall).

Lindert, Peter H., and Pugel, Thomas A., 1996. *International Economics* (Boston, Ma.: Irwin McGraw-Hill)

Levy, Jack S., 1999. "Contending Theories of International Conflict. A levels-of-Analysis Approach". In Crocker, Chester; Hampson, Fen Osler with Aal, Pamela, *Managing Global Chaos. Sources and Responses to International Conflict, Fourth Edition* (Washington D.C.: United States Institute for Peace Press).

Lindberg, Leon, 1963. *The Political Dynamics of European Economic Integration* (Stanford: Stanford University Press).

Lindberg, Leon, and Scheingold, Stuart A., 1971. *Regional Integration: Theory and Research* (Cambridge, Mass.: Harvard University Press).

Linz, Juan J., 1978. *The Breakdown of Democratic Regimes, Crisis, Breakdown and Reequilibration* (Baltimore: The Johns Hopkins University Press).

Linz, Juan, and Stepan, Alfred, 1996. *Problems of Transitions and Democratic Consolidation* (Baltimore: The Johns Hopkins University Press).

Looney, Robert, and Frederiksen, Peter C., 2000. "The Effect of Declining Military Influence of Defense Budgets in Latin America". *Armed Forces and Society*, Vol. 26, No. 3, Spring: 437-449.

Loveman, Brian,
----1991. "Misión Cumplida? Civil Military Relations and the Chilean Political Transition". *Journal of Interamerican Studies and World Affairs*, Vol. 33, No.3, Fall: 35-74.
----1994. "Protected Democracies and Military Guardianships: Political Transition in Latin America, 1978-1993. *Journal of Interamerican Studies and World Affairs*, Vol. 36, No. 2, Summer 1994: 105-189.

Lowenthal, Abraham, 1999. "United States and Latin American Relations at the Century's Turn: Managing the Intermestic Agenda". In Fishlow, Albert, and Jones,. James (Eds.), *The United States and the Americas. A Twenty-First Century View* (New York: W.W. Norton & Company).

Mahon, James E. Jr., 1992 (2000). "Was Latin America Too Rich to Prosper? Structural and Political Obstacles to Export-Led Industrial Growth". In Friedden, Jeffrey; Pastor, Manuel Jr.; and Tomz, Michael (Eds.), *Modern Political Economy and Latin America. Theory and Policy* (Boulder: Westview Press).

Mally, Gerhard, 1973. *The European Community in Perspective. The New Europe, the United States, and the World* (Lexington, Ma.: Lexington Books).

Mani Clark, Cristina, 2000. "Concepciones de la Defensa Nacional en Argentina y Chile: Una comparación de los Libros de la Defensa". *Fuerzas Armadas y Sociedad,* Año 15, No. 2, abril-junio.

Mansfield, Edward D., and Snyder, Jack, 1995. "Democratization and the Danger of War". *International Security*, Vol. 20., No. 1 (Summer): 5-38.

Manzetti, Luigi, 1993-94. "The Political Economy of Mercosur". *Journal of Interamerican Studies and World Affairs*. Vol. 35, No. 4, Winter: 101-41.

Maoz, Zeev, 1997. "The Controversy Over the Democratic Peace. Rearguard Action or Cracks in the Wall?". *International Security*, Vol. 22, No. 1, Summer: 162-98.

Marcella, Gabriel, 1995. *War and Peace in the Amazon: Strategic Implications for the Unites States and Latin America of the 1995 Ecuador-Peru War*. Monograph, Strategic Studies Institute, U.S. Army, November 24.

Markwald, Ricardo, and Machado, Joao Bosco, 1999. "Establishing an Industrial Policy for Mercosur". In Roett, Riordan (Ed.), *MERCOSUR. Regional Integration, World Markets* (Boulder, CO.: Lynne Rienner Publishers).

Mares, David, 1994. "Inter-American Security Communities: Concepts and Challenges". In Schoultz, Lars; Smith, William; and Varas, Augusto (Eds.), *Security, Democracy and Development in U.S.-Latin American Relations* (Miami: North South Center Press, University of Miami).

Mares, David R., and Bernstein, Steven A., 1998. "The Use of Force in Latin American Interstate Relations". In Domínguez, Jorge (Ed.), *International Security and Democracy. Latin America and the Caribbean in the Post Cold War Era* (Pittsburgh: Pittsburgh University Press).

McCormick, John, 1999. *Understanding the European Union* (London: Palgrave).

McMillan, Susan M. "Interdependence and Conflict". *Mershon International Studies Review*, Vol. 41, Supplement 1, May: 33-58.
McSherry, J. Patrice, 1997. *Incomplete Transition. Military Power and Democracy in Argentina* (New York: St. Martin's Press).

Mearshimer, John J., 1995. "The False Promise of International Institutions". Reprinted in Brown, Michael E.; Coté, Owen R. Jr.; Lynn –Jones, Sean M.; and Miller, Steven E. (Eds.), *Theories of War and Peace. An International Security Reader* (Cambridge: The MIT Press, 2000).

Meirelles, Carlos, 2000. *Antología Geopolítica de Autores Militares Chilenos* (Santiago: Centro de Estudios e Investigaciones Militares).

Meneses, Emilio,
----1989. *El Factor Naval en las Relaciones Entre Chile y los Estados Unidos (1881-1951)* (Santiago: Hachette).
----1993. "Percepciones de Amenazas Militares y Agenda Para la Política de Defensa". In Cruz Johnson, Rigoberto, and Varas, Augusto, *Percepciones de Amenaza y Políticas de Defensa en América Latina* (Santiago: FLACSO-Chile/Centro de Estudios Estratégicos de la Armada de Chile).

Meneses, Emilio, and Navarro, Miguel, 1989. "Política de Defensa: el caso de la adquisición de sistemas de Armas". Centro de Estudios Públicos, *Documento de Trabajo No. 121*, Santiago.

Milet, Paz, 1999. "Posicionamiento de los actores chilenos frente al proceso de integración". In Rojas A., Francisco (Ed.) 1999. *Argentina, Brasil y Chile: Integracion y Seguridad* (Santiago: FLACSO-Chile/Nueva Sociedad).

Milet, Paz; Fuentes, Claudio; and Rojas, Francisco, 1997. "Introducción: El MERCOSUR, Nuevo Actor Internacional". In Milet, Paz; Gaspar, Gabriel; and Rojas A., Francisco (Eds.), *Chile-MERCOSUR: Una alianza Estratégica* (Santiago: FLASO-Chile).

Mitchell, Christopher, 2000. "The Future of Migration as an Inter American issue". In Domínguez, Jorge I. (Ed.), *The Future of Inter-American Relations* (New York: Routledge).

Mitrany, David, 1965. "The Prospects of Integration: Federal or Functional?". *Journal of Common Market Studies* 4, December: 119-49.

Molina Johnson, Carlos, Chilean Army General, 2000. "Cooperación Regional: Potencialidades y limitaciones desde la perspectiva de la defensa nacional". *Fuerzas Armadas y Sociedad*, Año 15, No. 2, Abril-Junio: 26-38.

Mols, Manfred, 1996. "Regional Integration and the International System". In Smith, Peter H., and Nishijima, Shoji, (Eds.), *Cooperation or Rivalry? Regional Integration in the Americas and the Pacific Rim* (Boulder: Westview Press).

Moravcsik, Andrew,
----1991. "Negotiating the Single European Act". In Keohane, Robert O., and Hoffman, Stanley. *The New European Community. Decisionmaking and Institutional Change* (Boulder: Westview Press).
----1993. "Preferences and Power in the European Community: A Liberal Intergovernmentalist Approach". *Journal of Common Market Studies*, Vol. 31, No. 4, December: 473-524.
----1995. "Liberal Intergovernmentalism and Integration: A Rejoinder". *Journal of Common Market Studies*, Vol. 33, No. 4, December: 611-28.

Muñoz, Heraldo
----1996a. "The Dominant Themes in Latin American Foreign Relations: An Introduction". In Muñoz, Heraldo, and Tulchin, Joseph S. (Eds.), *Latin American Notions in World Politics. Second Edition* (Boulder: Westview Press).
----1996b. "Collective Action for democracy in the Americas". In Muñoz, Heraldo, and Tulchin, Joseph S. (Eds.), *Latin American Notions in World Politics. Second Edition* (Boulder: Westview Press).
----2000. "Toward a Regime for Advancing Democracy in the Americas". In Domínguez, Jorge I., (Ed.), *The Future of Inter-American Relations* (Baltimore: The Johns Hopkins University Press).

Murray, Williamson, 1997. "Clausewitz Out, Computer In. Military Culture and Technological Hubris". *The National Interest*, Summer 1997: 57-64.

Murray, Williamson, and Grimsley, Mark, 1999 (1994). "Introduction: On Strategy". In Murray, Williamson; Knox, MacGregor; and Bernstein, Alvin (Eds.), *The Making of Strategy* (Cambridge: Cambridge University Press).

Neuman, Stephanie G., 1998. "International Relations Theory and the Third World: An Oxymoron?". In Neuman, Stephanie G. (Ed.), 1998. *International Relations Theory and the Third World* (New York: St. Martin's Press).

Nohlen, Dieter, 1996. *Democracia, Transición y Gobernabilidad* (México, D.F.: Instituto Federal Electoral).

Nunn, Frederick M., 1976. *The Military in the Chilean History. Essays on Civil-Military Relations, 1810-1973.* (Albuquerque: University of New Mexico Press)

Nye, Joseph S. Jr., 1971 (1987). *Peace in Parts. Integration and Conflict in Regional Organization* (Lanham: University Press of America).

O'Donnell, Guillermo,
----1973 (1986). "Modernization and Bureaucratic-Authoritarianism. Studies in South American Politics". Reprinted in Peter F. Klarén and Thomas J. Bossert (Eds.), *Promise of Development. Theories of Change in Latin America* (Boulder/London: Westview Press).
----1994 (1999). "Delegative Democracy". Journal of Democracy, Vol. 5, No. 1. Reprinted in O'Donnell, Guillermo, *Counterpoints. Selected Essays on Authoritarianism and Democratization* (Notre Dame: University of Notre Dame Press).

Owen, John M., 1994 (2000). "How Liberalism Produces Democratic Peace". Reprinted in Brown, Michael E.; Coté, Owen R. Jr.; Lynn –Jones, Sean M.; and Miller, Steven E. (Eds.), *Theories of War and Peace. An International Security Reader* (Cambridge: The MIT Press, 2000).

Owen, William, ADM, 1996. "The Emerging System of Systems". *Armed Forces Journal*, (January): 47.

Pastor, Manuel, and Wise, Carol, 1999. "The Politics of Second-Generation Reform". *Journal of Democracy*, Vol. 10, No. 3: 34-48.

Pérez, Edmundo, 1997. *Los Desafíos de Seguridad y Defensa en el MERCOSUR* (Buenos Aires: SER en el 2000 Online Database).

Peña, Felix, 1999. "Broadening and Deepening: Striking the Right Balance". In Roett, Riordan (Ed.), *MERCOSUR. Regional Integration, World Markets* (Boulder, CO.: Lynne Rienner Publishers).

Pike, Frederick B., 1963. *Chile and the United States. The Emergence of Chile's Social Crisis and the Challenge to United States Diplomacy* (Notre Dame: University of Notre Dame Press).

Pion-Berlin, David,
----1999. *Civil-Military Circumvention: How Argentine State Institutions Compensate for a Weakened Chain of Command.* Paper prepared for delivery at the Soldier and Democracy in Latin America Conference. February 19-20, 1999, Mission Inn, Riverside, California.
----2000. "Will Soldiers Follow? Economic Integration and Regional Security in the Southern Cone. *Journal of Interamerican Studies and World Affairs*: 43-67.

Przeworski, Adam, 1991. *Democracy and the Market. Political and Economic Reforms in Eastern Europe and Latin America* (Cambridge: Cambridge University Press).

Puchala, Donald, J.,
----1972. "Of Blind Men, Elephants, and Regional Integration". *Journal of Common Market Studies* Vol. 10, No. 3: 267-84.
---1998. "Institutionalism, Intergovernmentalism and European Integration: A review Article". *Journal of Common Market Studies* Vol. 37, No. 2, June: 317-31.

Putnam, Robert D., 1988. "Diplomacy and domestic politics: the logic of two-level games" *International Organization*, Vol. 42, No. 3, Summer: 427-60.

Quintana, Germán, 1997. "Corredores de Integración Física Internacional". In Milet, Paz; Gaspar, Gabriel; and Rojas A., Francisco (Eds.), *Chile-MERCOSUR: Una alianza Estratégica* (Santiago: FLASO-Chile).
Quintero, Neile, 200. "Chile". IADB Country Report 2000. Available online at [http://www.iadb.org/int/sta/ENGLISH/staweb/#regrpt], accessed April 23, 2001.

Radelet, Steven, and Sachs, Jeffrey, 1997. "Asia's Reemergence". *Foreign Affairs*, November/December 1997: 44-59

Remmer, Karen L.,
----1995. "New Theoretical Perspectives on Democratization". *Comparative Politics* Vol. 28, No. 1: 103-22.
----1996. "External Pressures and Domestic Constrains. The Lessons of the Four Case Studies". In Farer, Tom (Ed.), *Beyond Sovereignty. Collectively Defending Democracy in the Americas* (Baltimore: The Johns Hopkins University Press).

Rizzo de Oliveira, Eliezer, 1999. "El caso brasileno: la política de defensa nacional y la seguridad regional". In Rojas A., Francisco, *Argentina, Brasil y Chile: Integracion y Seguridad* (Santiago: FLACSO-Chile/Nueva Sociedad, 2000).

Robledo, Marcos,

----1997. "Sector Privado, Política Exterior y Estrategia de Inserción Económica Internacional". In Milet, Paz; Gaspar, Gabriel; and Rojas A., Francisco (Eds.), *Chile-MERCOSUR: Una alianza Estratégica* (Santiago: FLASO-Chile).
----2001 (Forthcoming). "Relaciones civiles-militares y adquisiciones militares en Chile, 1924-2000". (Santiago: FLACSO-Chile).

Rojas A., Francisco,
----1992. "Cooperación Para la Seguridad Hemisférica: Construyendo la Seguridad Cooperativa". *Fuerzas Armadas y Sociedad* VII: 1-13.
----1994. "Security Regimes in the Western Hemisphere: A View from Latin America". In Schoultz, Lars; Smith, Williams; and Varas, Augusto F. (Eds.), *Security, Democracy and Development in U.S. Latin American Relations* (Miami: North-South Center Press, University of Miami).
----(Ed.), 1998. *Globalización, América Latina y la Diplomacia de Cumbres* (Santiago: FLACSO-Chile).
----1998a. "Transition and Civil-Military relations in Chile. Contributions in a New International Framework". In Domínguez, Jorge (Ed.), *International Security and Democracy. Latin America and the Caribbean in the Post-Cold War Era* (Pittsburgh: University of Pittsburgh Press).
----(Ed.) 1999. *Argentina, Brasil y Chile: Integracion y Seguridad* (Santiago: FLACSO-Chile/Nueva Sociedad).

Rosales, Osvaldo, 2000. "Chile-Mercosur: los Pasos hacia la Integración". *Análisis del Mes*, Dirección de Relaciones Económicas Internacionales, Ministerio de Relaciones Exteriores de Chile, Octubre, available at [www.direcon.cl/analisis/del_mes/amalisismerco.htm], accessed Novembr 17, 2000.

Rotfeld, Adam Daniel, 1999. "Rethinking the contemporary security system". *SIPRI Yearbook 1999. Armaments, Disarmament and International Security* (Oxford: Oxford University Press).

Rouquié, Alain, 1987 (1982). *The Military and the State in Latin America* (Berkeley: University of California Press).

Saavedra Rivano, Neandro, 1996. "Chile and the Regional Integration". In Nishijima, Shoji, and Smith, Peter H., (Eds.), *Cooperation or Rivalry? Regional Integration in the Americas and the Pacific Rim* (Boulder, CO: Westview Press).

Sachs, Jeffrey D., 1985 (2000). "External Debt and Macroeconomic Performance in Latin America and East Asia". In Frieden, Jeffrey; Pastor, Manuel Jr.; and Tomz, Michael (Eds.), *Modern Political Economy and Latin America. Theory and Policy* (Boulder: Westview Press).

Saín, Marcelo Fabian, 1999. "Seguridad Regional, Defensa Nacional y Relaciones Cívico-Militares en Argentina". In Rojas, Francisco, *Argentina, Brasil y Chile: Integragion y Seguridad* (Santiago: FLACSO-Chile/Nueva Sociedad).

Sandholtz, Wayne, and Zyman, John, 1989. "Recasting the European Bargain". *World Politics*, Vol. XLII, No. 1, October.

Scheetz, Thomas, 1998. "La Ley de Reestructuración Militar Argentina: la Triste Continuación de una Política Militar Gatopardista". In Diamint, Rut, (Ed.), *Argentina y la Seguridad Internacional* (Santiago: FLACSO-Chile/W.Wilson Center)

Schmitter, Philippe C., 1991. "Change in Regime Type and Progress in International Relations". In Adler, Emanuel, and Crawford, Beverly (Eds.), *Progress in Postwar International Relations* (New York: Columbia University Press).

Schwartz, Gilson, 1996. "Brazil, Mercosur and SAFTA: destructive restructuring or Pan-American Integration?". In Smith, Peter H., and Nishijima, Shoji (Eds.), 1996. *Cooperation or Rivalry? Regional Integration in the Americas and the Pacific Rim* (Boulder, CO: Westview Press).

Sheahan, John, 1999. *Searching for a Better Society. The Peruvian Economy From 1950* (University Park, PS.: The Pennsylvania State University Press).

Sheahan, John, and Iglesias, Enrique, 1998. "Kinds and Causes of Inequality in Latin America". In Birdsall, Nancy; Graham, Carol; and Sabot, Richard H., (Eds.), *Beyond Tradeoffs: Market reform and Equitable Growth in Latin America* (Washington, D.C.: Inter-American Development Bank/Brookings Institution Press.

Skidmore, Thomas E., and Smith, Peter H., 1997. *Modern Latin America. Fourth Edition* (Oxford: Oxford University Press).

Smith, Peter, 2000. *Talons of the Eagle. Dynamics of U.S.-Latin American Relations* (New York: Oxford University Press).

Smith, Peter H., and Nishijima, Shoji, (Eds.), *Cooperation or Rivalry? Regional Integration in the Americas and the Pacific Rim* (Boulder: Westview Press).

Soares de Lima, María Regina,
----1996. "Brazil's Response to the 'New Regionalism'". In Mace, Gordon, and Thérien, Jean-Philippe, *Foreign Policy and Regionalism in the Americas* (Boulder: Lynne Rienner Publishers).
----1999. "Brazil's Alternative Vision". In Mace, Gordon, and Bélanger, Louis, *The Americas in Transition. The Contours of Regionalism"* (Boulder: Lynne Rienner).

Somavía, Juan, and Insulza, Jose Miguel, 1990. *Seguridad Democratica Regional: una Concepcion Alternativa* (Caracas: Nueva Sociedad).

St. John, Ronald Bruce, 1992. *The Foreign Policy of Peru* (Boulder: Lynne Rienner Publishers).

Stallings, Barbara, and Peres, Wilson, 2000. *Growth, Employment, and Equity. The Impact of the Economic Reforms in Latin America and the Caribbean* (Washington D.C.: United Nations Economic Commission for Latin America and the Caribbean/ Brookings Institution Press).

Thelen, Kathleen, and Steimo, Sven, 1002. "Historical institutionalism in comparative perspective". In Steimo, Sven; Thelen, Kathleen; and Longstreth, Frank, *Structuring Politics. Historical institutionalism in comparative analysis* (Cambridge: Cambridge University Press).

Stepan, Alfred,
----1973. "The new Professionalism of Internal Warfare and Military Role Expansion". In Stepan, Alfred (Ed.), *Authoritarian Brazil* (New Haven: Yale University Press).
----1978. *The State and Society: Peru in Comparative Perspective* (Princeton: Princeton University Press).
----1988. *Rethinking Military Politics. Brazil and the Southern Cone* (Princeton, N.J.: Princeton University Press).

Stockholm International Peace Research Institute (SIPRI). *SIPRI Yearbook 1999.Armaments, Disarmament and International Security* (Oxford: Oxford University Press).

Thurow, Lester, 1992. *Head to Head: The Coming Economic Battle Among Japan, Europe, and America* (New York: Morrow).

Tomassini, Luciano, 1985. "The Disintegration of the integration process: towards new forms of regional cooperation". In Gauhar, Altaf (Ed.), *Regional Integration: The Latin American Experience* (Boulder: Westview Press/Third World Foundation for Socioeconomic Studies).

Trinkunas, Harold A., 2000. "Crafting Civilian Control in Emerging Democracies: Argentina and Venezuela". *Journal of Interamerican Studies and World Affairs*, Vol. 42, No. 3 (Summer): 77-109.

Tsoulakis, Loukas, 2000. "Economic and Monetary Union. Political Conviction and Economic Uncertainty". In Wallace, Helen, and Wallace, William, *Policy-Making in the European Union* (Oxford: Oxford University Press).

Tulchin, Joseph S., Rojas A., Francisco (Eds.), and Espach, Ronald, 1998. *Strategic Balance and Confidence Building Measures in the Americas* (Washington D.C./Stanford, CA.: The W. Wilson Center Press/Stanford University Press).

Urriola, Rafael, and Rebolledo, Andrés, 1998. "Regionalismo, Multuilateralismo y Coordinación Macroeconómica". In Rojas A., Francisco (Ed.), 1998. *Globalización, América Latina y la Diplomacia de Cumbres* (Santiago: FLACSO-Chile).

Valenzuela, Arturo,

----1997. "Paraguay: The Coup That Didn't Happen". *Journal of Democracy*, Vol. 8, No. 1, January: 43-55.

----1999. "Chile: Origins and Consolidation of a Latin American Democracy". In Diamond, Larry; Hartlyn, Jonathan; Linz, Juan J.; and Lipset, Seymour Martin (Eds.), 1999. *Democracy in Developing Countries. Latin America. Second Edition* (Boulder, CO.: Lynne Rienner Publishers).

Valls Pereira, Lia, 1999. "Toward the Common Market of the South: Mercosur's Origins, Evolution, and Challenges". In Roett, Riordan (Ed.), *MERCOSUR. Regional Integration, World Markets* (Boulder, CO.: Lynne Rienner Publishers).

Varas, Augusto,

----1993. "La Post Guerra Fría, la Seguridad Hemisférica y la Defensa Nacional". In Varas, Augusto and Cruz J., Rigoberto, *Percepciones de Amenaza y Políticas de Defensa en América del Sur* (Santiago: FLACSO-Chile).

----1994a. "Post-Cold War Security Interests and perceptions of Threat in the Western Hemisphere". In Schoultz, Lars; Smith, Williams; and Varas, Augusto F. (Eds.), *Security, Democracy and Development in U.S. Latin American Relations* (Miami: North-South Center Press, University of Miami).

----1994b. "La Seguridad Hemisférica Cooperativa de Post-Guerra Fría". *Serie Relaciones Internacionales y Política Exterior*, N° 3, Agosto, Santiago, FLACSO-Chile.

Van Klaveren, Alberto,

----1996. "Understanding Latin American Foreign Policies". In Muñoz, Heraldo, and Tulchin, Joseph S. (Eds.), *Latin American Notions in World Politics. Second Edition* (Boulder: Westview Press).

----1997. "Inserción Internacional de Chile". In Lahera, Eugenio, and Toloza, Cristian (Eds.), *Chile en los Noventa* (Santiago: Dolmen).

Varas, Augusto; Agüero, Felipe; y Bustamante, Fernando, 1980. *Chile, Democracia y Fuerzas Armadas* (Santiago: FLACSO-Chile).

Varas, Augusto, y Caro, Isaac, 1994. *Medidas de Confianza Mutua en América Latina* (Santiago: FLACSO-Chile/Stimson Center/SER).

Vieira, G., General, 1994. "La variable estratégica en el proceso de constitutión del MERCOSUR". *Revista Seguridad Estratégica regional* 5 (March): 8-13.

Von Chrismar Escutti, Julio, 1968 (2000). "Leyes que se deducen del estudio de la expansión de los estados". In Meirelles, Carlos, *Antología Geopolítica de Autores Militares Chilenos* (Santiago: Centro de Estudios e Investigaciones Militares, 2000).

Waisman, Carlos H., 1999. "Argentina: Capitalism and Democracy". In Diamond, Larry; Hartlyn, Jonathan; Linz, Juan J.; and Lipset, Seymour Martin (Eds.). *Democracy in*

*Developing Countries. Latin America. Second Edition* (Boulder, CO.: Lynne Rienner Publishers).

Wallace, Helen, 2000. "Analyzing and Explaining Policies". In Wallace, Helen, and Wallace, William, *Policy-Making in the European Union* (Oxford: Oxford University Press).

Wallace, William, 2000. "Collective Governance". In Wallace, Helen, and Wallace, William, *Policy-Making in the European Union* (Oxford: Oxford University Press).

Walt, Stephen , 1987. *The Origins of Alliances* (Ithaca: Cornell University Press, 1987).

Waltz, Kenneth,
----1959. *Man, the State, and War* (New York: Columbia University Press).
----1979. *Theory of International Politics* (New York: McGraw-Hill).

Weber, Max, 1919 (1958). "Politics as a Vocation". In Gerth, H. H., and Mills, C. Wright. *From Max Weber: Essays in Sociology* (Oxford: Oxford University Press).

Weidner, Glenn R., 2000. *Challenges to the third wave of democratization in Latin America: the military dimension.* Paper prepared for the Conference on Challenges to Democracy in the Americas. The Carter Center. Washington, D.C., September 20, 2000.

Wendt, Alexander, 1992. "Anarchy is What States Make of It: The Social Construction of power politics". *International Organization*, Vol. 46, No. 2, Spring: 391-425).

Williamson, John, 1990. "The Progress of Reform Policy in Latin America". In Williamson, John (Ed.), *Latin American Adjustment: How Much Has Happened?* (Washington D.C.: Institute for International Studies).

Zaverucha, Jorge, 1998. *Sarney, Collor, Itamar, FHC e as Prerogativas Militares (1985-1998).* Paper prepared for delivery at the 1998 meeting of the Latin American Studies Association, The Palmer Hilton House Hotel, Chicago, Illinois, September 24-26, 1998.

THIS PAGE INTENTIONALLY LEFT BLANK

# APPENDIX. EVOLUTION OF MERCOSUR'S PRESIDENTIAL AGENDA OF POLITICAL CONCERTATION 1991-2001.

(Source: Mercosur 2001).

| Year | International | Political | Security |
|------|-------------|-----------|----------|
| 1991 | Mercosur agrees to coordinate positions in:<br>• Multilateral economic forum (Cairns group).<br>• The 1992 U.N. Conference on Sustainable Development at Rio de Janeiro.<br>• To study a cooperation agreement with the European Union. | Treaty of Asunción creates Mercosur. Intra-regional free trade liberalization begins. | Mercosur congratulates Argentina because its signature of the Safeguards Agreements with the AIEA. |
| 1992 | Mercosur – EU first inter-institutional agreement.<br><br>Mercosur declares a successful end of the GATT Uruguay Round as "indispensable" for the economic growth of Mercosur economies. | Mercosur declares that democratic institutions are indispensable for its existence and development | |
| 1993 | Mercosur presidents declare their concern regarding the increase in protectionism measures adopted by the biggest world economies. | Mercosur's inter-parliamentary cooperation begins. | |
| 1994 | Mercosur approves Brazilian proposal within the Rio Group to advance toward a South American Free Trade Area.<br><br>Mercosur welcomes Bolivia as observer into the group.<br><br>Mercosur celebrates the end of the GATT Uruguay Round and underlines the close coordination between its members during the negotiations. | Mercosur confirms that integration consolidates domestic democratic processes. | |
| 1995 | Bolivia and Chile begins negotiations to create a Mercosur+2 free trade area.<br><br>Mercosur welcomes the First Summit of the Americas, asserting that there is a "perfect compatibility between the hemispheric and Mercosur's chronograms.<br><br>Mercosur welcomes the EU decision to reach a framework agreement with | Treaty of Ouro Preto establishes the customs union since January 1st 1995 and the institutional structure of Mercosur. It includes:<br>-The Council of the Common Market (Presidents or Ministers of Foreign Affairs).<br>-Regular meetings of Ministers of Economy and Presidents of Central Banks, (since 1995), Agriculture, Education, Justice, Labor, Culture (1995), health (1995), Interior | |

| | | | |
|---|---|---|---|
| | the group.<br><br>Mercosur assumes legal personality under international law, establishing formal relations with several multilateral institutions. | (1996), Industry (1997), Mines and Energy (2000), and Social Development (2000).<br><br>Mercosur reaffirms that democratic values are essential for the creation of the common market.<br><br>Mercosur asserts that the customs union introduces a new political dimension seeking for a "wide and deep " integration.<br><br>Mercosur asserts that integration trascends its economic and commercial aspects, encompassing a growing nukber of areas, such as education, science technology, justice, environment, physical infrastructure and communications. | |
| 1996 | Chilean and Bolivian Presidents begin to meet Mercosur leaders in 4+2 format, parallel to Mercosur Council of the Common Market.<br><br>The Mercosur-Chilean free trade zone begins to operate.<br><br>Mercosur adopts the 2000 Action Program, which includes multiple negotiations and political dialogs, providing "a world perspective to the foreign agenda of Mercosur", such as:<br>-The FTAA<br>-The Andean Community<br>-Mexico<br>-The EU<br>-Central America and the Caribbean<br>-Australia and new Zealand<br>-The Russian Federation<br>-Japan<br>-India<br><br>Mercosur establishes a **Mechanism of Political Consultation and Concertation** through the "Presidential Declaration on Political Dialogue", among which goals are:<br>-To examine international issues of special relevance for states parties aiming to concert positions regarding to them.<br>-To consider affairs of common political interest related to third countries, groups of countries or international organizations. | Mercosur adopts the **"Presidential Declaration About the Democratic Compromise"**, conditioning the membership to the group to the full validity of democratic institutions.<br><br>Mercosur presidents reaffirm their full adherence to the democratic principles and institutions, to the state of law, the respect of human rights, and to the basic liberties.<br><br>Mercosur establishes a **"Mechanism of Political consultation and Concertation"** through the "Presidential Declaration on Political Dialogue", aimed to:<br><br>-Enlarge and systematize political cooperation among states parties. | Mercosur + 2 presidents state their support for Argentine rights and claims over the "Malvinas Islands". |
| 1997 | Bolivia-Mercosur agreement begins to operate. | Decision No. 12/97 incorporates Chile (and Bolivia) to the Forum | Presidents instruct Ministers of Justice to accelerate the |

| | | | |
|---|---|---|---|
| | Mercosur states to be a "strategic alliance to face and take advantage of the challenges of globalization and ease the insertion of the states in the international context".<br><br>Peru and Mexico begin negotiations regarding free trade agreements with Mercosur (4 + 1).<br><br>Adds political dialogue with China and the Commonwealth of Independent States to its foreign agenda.<br><br>Mercosur coordinates its positions at the Third Trade Ministerial of the Americas at Belo Horizonte (Brazil) regarding the U.S. posture in relation to the FTAA. | and all the Mercosur's institutions, but when "both parties" agree on that. Article 6 establishes that Mercosur and Chile "will establish regular coordination in all those negotiations of interesting to both parties, including external missions".<br><br>States that the development and deepening of integration have a growing political dimension, which demands coordinated and systematized actions of the partners.<br><br>States that democratic regimes as "essential condition for cooperation", and alteration of democratic order as "unacceptable" for the continuity of the affected member within the integration process. | harmonization of domestic law between Mercosur +2 "in all the areas of the fight against organized crime. |
| 1998 | Mercosur agrees on the Second Summit of the Americas to begin negotiations aimed to "conclude the negotiation of the FTAA no later than 2005"[130].<br><br>Mercosur + 2 meets with South African President, Nelson Mandela in July 24, Ushuaia (Argentina).<br><br>Mercosur and the Andean Community sign a framework agreement for the creation of an free trade zone (April 16).<br><br>Mercosur reaches agreements:<br>-On investment with the Central American Common Market (April 18).<br>-On investment and trade with Canada (June).<br><br>Mercosur begins talks with South Korea. | Mechanism of Political Consultation and Concertation is replaced by the **Forum for Consultation and Concertation.**<br><br>Mercosur, Bolivia and Chile subscribe the "Protocol of Ushuaia About the Democratic Compromise", which incorporates the democratic clause as part of the Treaty of Asunción and the Treaties between Mercosur, Bolivia and Chile.<br><br>Mercosur adopts the "Social-Labor Declaration" and agrees on a policy regarding consumer's rights. | Mercosur, Bolivia and Chile adopt the "Political Declaration of Mercosur, Bolivia and Chile as Zone of Peace". The document sates that:<br>-Peace is essential to develop and continue regional integration.<br>-To strengthen the mechanisms of consultation and cooperation on security and defense issues currently existing between its members and to **promote their progressive articulation**.<br>-To make efforts at international forums to advance in international agreements aimed to achieve nuclear disarmament and non-proliferation in all of its aspects. |
| 1999 | Mercosur underlines the importance on maintaining a cohesive position in foreign relations.<br><br>First Mercosur-European Union Summit held at Rio de Janeiro (June). Mercosur agrees to begin negotiations with the EU and to finish them before | Brazil modifies its exchange rate policy toward free floatation (January)<br><br>Mercosur creates a working group to prepare alternative plans for macroeconomic coordination aimed to gradual convergence of | Uruguay, on behalf of Mercosur, intervenes at the LIV U.N. General Assembly (October), expressing concern about the transit of radioactive material through sea-lanes of communication close to territorial waters and/or |

---

[130] Summit of the Americas (1998).

| | | | |
|---|---|---|---|
| | 2005. | domestic public policies. | Economic Exclusive Zone. |
| | Mercosur agrees to act jointly in the next World Trade Organization (WTO) round, especially focused on agricultural liberalization. | Mercosur establishes its ad-hoc arbitral courts in Paraguay after reaching the Brasilia Protocol on controversy resolution. | |
| | Mercosur reaches an agreement on investment with Australia and new Zealand. | | |
| | Mercosur expresses its concern because the lack of advances at the WTO Ministerial at Seattle. | | |
| 2000 | Mercosur, Bolivian and Chilean Presidents agreed on:<br>-To advance toward growing Bolivian and Chilean incorporation to Mercosur.<br>-Highlight the coincidences reached by their governments regarding the coordination and concertation of position at forums and international organizations, consolidating their "regional role in the international scene", underlining the role of the Forum of Political Consultation and Concertation for the integration process and for the political dialogue with other regions.<br>-Take note on the parallel advance of the Mercosur and Chilean negotiations toward association agreements.<br>-Highlight the 4+2 coordination reached regarding WTO negotiations.<br><br>Mercosur representatives agree on September to begin formal negotiations aiming to full Chilean incorporation to the group. Negotiations should begin at the December Florianapolis (Brazil) Presidential Summit.<br><br>Chile and the U.S. announce the beginning of bilateral negotiations toward a free trade agreement (September). Mercosur suspends negotiations with Chile[131].<br><br>Mercosur meets with South African | Mercosur Relaunching. Ministers of Commerce and President of Central banks of Mercosur, Bolivia and Chile agreed on a timetable of macroeconomic convergence.<br><br>Mercosur reaches an agreement on car trade and advances on the sugar regime.<br><br>Representatives of Mercosur, Bolivia, and Chile meet in Paraguay (March 21) aiming to concert policies and coordinate initiatives regarding human rights, particularly at international forums.<br><br>Members of the Chilean Congress are incorporated to the Mercosur Parliamentary Commission. | Presidents of Mercosur, Bolivia and Chile reaffirmed their commitment with disarmament and non-proliferation of weapons of mass destruction, and agree on:<br>-Support the advances on the Non-Proliferation Treaty (NPT) Review Conference.<br>-Support the advances of the ad hoc group of Biological and Toxin Weapons Convention (BTWC).<br>-Welcome the fact that all South American countries ratified the Chemical Weapons Convention (CWC).<br>-Underlined the importance of deepening efforts and initiatives toward transparency regarding conventional weapons, and called for an universal participation on the U.N. Conventional Weapons Registrar.<br>-Expressed their intention to promote common efforts against drug trafficking and transnational crime.<br><br>Ministers of Interior of Mercosur, Bolivia, and Chile, agree on plans for reciprocal cooperation and coordination regarding:<br>-Child traffic.<br>-Economic-financial crimes. |

---

[131] The freezing of the talks was first announced by Brazilian Foreign Affairs Minister Luiz Felipe Lampreia, and later formally confirmed by Group of the Common Market (the executive organ) during its meeting in Brasilia, December 9. Brazilian ambassador to Mercosur José Botafogo made the announcement on December 9, 2000, presenting it as a "period of reflexión". See El Mercurio (2000, 2000c).

| | | | |
|---|---|---|---|
| | President Thabo Mbeki and signs a framework agreement, beginning negotiations toward a free trade area.<br><br>Mercosur agrees to reach a free trade agreement with the Andean Community before 2002.<br><br>Mercosur begins talks with the European Free Trade Association (EFTA). | | -Illicit traffic on nuclear and/or radioactive material. |
| 2001 | | Argentina temporarily suspends the customs union[132]. | Argentina, Brazil, Chile, and Uruguay express their concern to France, Great Britain and Japan, about the transport of radioactive materials through Cape Horn. Also, the governments insisted on the necessity of further negotiations within international organizations toward more secure regimes of transportation norms[133]. |

---

[132] See The New York Times (2001).

[133] Ministerio de Relaciones Exteriores (2001d).

www.ingramcontent.com/pod-product-compliance
Lightning Source LLC
Chambersburg PA
CBHW080247290526
45790CB00005B/1731